Essays in the
Philosophy of History

R. G. Collingwood

British Library Cataloguing-in-Publication Data
A catalogue record for this book is available from the
British Library

R. G. Collingwood

Robin George Collingwood was born on 22nd February 1889, in Cartmel, England. He was the son of author, artist, and academic, W. G. Collingwood.

Collingwood attended Rugby School before enrolling at University College, Oxford, where he received a congratulatory first class honours for reading Greats. He became a fellow of Pembroke College, Oxford, and remained there for 15 years until he was offered the post of Waynflete Professor of Metaphysical Philosophy at Magdalen College, Oxford. He was greatly influenced by the Italian Idealists Croce, Gentile, and Guido de Ruggiero. Another important influence was his father, a professor of fine art and a student of Ruskin.

Collingwood produced *The Principles of Art* in 1938, outlining the concept of art as being essentially expressions of emotion. He claimed that it was a necessary function of the human mind and considered it an important collaborative activity. He also published other works of philosophy, such as *Speculum Mentis* (1924), *An Essay on Philosophic Method* (1933), *An Essay on Metaphysics* (1940), and many more. In 1940, he published *The First Mate's Log*, an account of a sailing trip he undertook with some of his students in the Mediterranean.

Collingwood died at Coniston, Lancashire on January 1943, after a series of debilitating strokes.

CONTENTS

ESSAYS

THE ESSAYS

Croce's Philosophy of History*

A N ALLIANCE between philosophy and history is no new idea
in this country. Most Englishmen who know or care anything
about philosophy have been influenced, directly or indirectly, by
the "Greats" school at Oxford; and the distinguishing mark of
this school is the connection which it maintains between the study
of ancient history and that of ancient philosophy. It is this connection that gives Oxford philosophy its chief merit, a fine tradition of scholarship and interpretation in Plato and Aristotle;
and it is, perhaps, the failure to extend the same principle to the
study of more recent thought that has led in this school to a much
lower standard in the interpretation of modern philosophy, un-
supported as it is by any study of modern history.

The ideal of a combined study of philosophy and history is
energetically supported by Croce. Himself a philosopher of
eminence and an accomplished historian, he feels acutely in his
own person the profit which each of his pursuits in turn derives
from the other. The historian must study the philosophy of his
period if he is to understand those forces which ultimately shaped
its destiny; if he does not follow the thoughts of the men whose

* Reprinted from *The Hibbert Journal* (1921), with the permission
of the editor.

actions he is studying he can never enter into the life of his period, and can at best observe it from outside as a sequence of unexplained facts, or facts to be explained by physical causes alone. And the philosopher must in his turn study history. How else is he to understand why certain problems at certain times pressed for solution on the philosopher's mind? How else is he to understand the individual philosopher's temperament, his out-look on life, the very symbolism and language in which he has expressed himself? In short, if the philosopher is to understand the history of philosophy he must study the general history of humanity; and a philosophy which ignores its own history is a philosophy which spends its labour only to rediscover errors long dead.

History without philosophy is history seen from the outside, the play of mechanical and unchanging forces in a materialist-ically conceived world: philosophy without history is philosophy seen from the outside, the veering and backing, rising and fall-ing, of motiveless winds of doctrine. "Both these are monsters." But history fertilised by philosophy is the history of the human spirit in its secular attempt to build itself a world of laws and in-stitutions in which it can live as it wishes to live; and philosophy fertilised by history is the progressive raising and solving of the endless intellectual problems whose succession forms the inner side of this secular struggle. Thus the two studies which, apart, degenerate into strings of empty dates and lists of pedantic dis-tinctions—"To seventeen add two, And Queen Anne you will view," "Barbara celarent darii ferioque prioris"—become, to-gether, a single science of all things human.

This is the point of view from which Croce proposes, and in his own work carries out, a closer union between philosophy and history. It is a point of view which must interest English readers; the more so as in these days, when the pre-eminence of classical studies in English education is a thing of the past, the position of philosophy as a subject of study demands the closest attention.

In the past the Oxford "Greats" school has stood for this ideal of the cross-fertilisation of history and philosophy, even when the coordination of the two sides has been worst, and the undergraduate has seemed to be merely reading two different schools at once, under tutors who regarded each other as rivals for his attention; but in the future the whole question will be reopened, and philosophy may either contract a new alliance with the natural sciences, or retire into single blessedness as an independent subject of study like Forestry or Geography, or force herself into the company of Modern History, disguised perhaps under the inoffensive name of Political Theory. To solve this problem in the best way it is necessary to have a clear idea of what philosophy is, and what are its relations to these other subjects of study. These, of course, are controversial questions, on which no one can lay down the law; but the conclusions of Croce demand at least our attention, and we propose here to discuss his views on the nature of history and its relation to philosophy. As our purpose is rather to criticise than to expound, we shall select some of his views and examine these as typical of the whole.

The book in which he expounds them is the *Teoria e Storia della Storiografia* (Bari, 1917), which, like many of Croce's books, falls into two sections, a theoretical and a historical. The relation between the two is close; the ideas which are discussed in the former are exemplified in the latter, and the process of development followed in the latter is only intelligible in the light of the principles laid down in the former. Our concern here is especially with the theoretical section; not because it is the most striking—the historical section is a rapid but extremely brilliant survey of the progress of historical thought, in which the characteristics of succeeding periods are set forth with a penetration and fairness which could hardly be bettered—but because our present business is the explicit statement of theoretical principles.

In order to arrive at a clear concept of what history is, Croce begins by telling us what it is not. It is not annals. That is to say, it is not the lists of dates with which a superficial observer confuses it. To the outward eye, a book may consist of mere chronological tables; but to the historian these tables mean real history, not because they are, but because they stand for, the thought which is history. History goes on in the mind of the historian: he thinks it, he enacts it within himself: he identifies himself with the history he is studying and actually lives it as he thinks it, whence Croce's paradox that "all history is contemporary history." Annals, on the other hand, belong to the past; the schoolboy learning a list of dates does not live them in his thought, but takes them as something alien imposed upon him from outside—brute facts, dead and dry; no living reality such as his teacher, if he is a good historian, can enjoy in reading the same list. Annals, then, are past history, and therefore not history at all. They are the dry bones of history, its dead,corpse.

This is illuminating, and satisfactory enough until we begin to reflect upon it. History is thought, annals the corpse of thought. But has thought a corpse? and if so, what is it like? The corpse of an organism is something other than the organism itself: what, for an idealistic philosopher like Croce, is there other than thought, in terms of which we can give a philosophically satisfactory definition of the corpse of thought?

Croce's general "philosophy of the spirit" supplies him with a ready-made answer. Nothing exists but the spirit; but the spirit has two sides or parts, thought and will. Whatever is not thought is will. If you find some fact which cannot be explained as an instance of thought, you must explain it as an instance of will. Thought is the synthesis of subject and object, and its characteristic is truth: will is the creation of an object by the subject, and its characteristic is utility. Wherever you find something which appears at first sight to be an example of thinking, but which on inspection is found not to possess the quality of truth, it follows that it must be an example of willing, and possess the quality of

CROCE'S PHILOSOPHY OF HISTORY
7

usefulness. Such, in a rough outline, is the principle of analysis which Croce applies in this book and elsewhere. History is thought: there is here a perfect synthesis of subject and object, inasmuch as the historian thinks himself into the history, and the two become contemporary. Annals are not thought but willed; they are constructed—"drawn up"—by the historian for his own ends; they are a convention serving the purposes of historical thought, as musical notation serves the purposes of musical thought without being musical thought; they are not true but useful.

This is the answer which Croce gives, or rather tries to give, to the question we raised. But he does not really succeed in giving it. He cannot bring himself to say that annals are simply devoid of truth, are in no sense an act of thought. That would amount to saying that annals are the words, and history their meaning: which would not be what he wanted. So he says that annals are (p. 9) "sounds, or graphic symbols representing sounds, held together and maintained not by an act of thought which thinks them (in which case they would once more be supplied with content), but by an act of will which thinks it useful for certain purposes of its own to preserve these words, empty or half empty though they be." "Or half empty." This is a strange reservation. Are the words of which annals are composed, then, not empty after all? Are they half full, half full, that is, of thought? But if so, the distinction between the act of thought and the act of will has broken down: annals are only history whose words mean less indeed than the same words as used by history proper, but still have meaning, are still essentially vehicles of thought. And Croce would be the first to admit and insist that a difference of degree has nothing to do with a philosophical question like this.

This is not the only passage in which Croce's clearness of vision and common sense break through the abstractions of his formal philosophy. He tries to maintain a philosophy according to which every act of the spirit falls under either one or the other of two mutually exclusive heads (theoretical and practical), subdivided into four sub-heads (intuition and thought; economic willing and ethical willing), so related that the second and fourth sub-heads involve the first and third respectively (thought is also intuition, ethical action is also economic action), but not *vice versa*. Now this formal philosophy of the mind is purely psychological and empirical in character; it is what Croce himself calls "naturalism" or "transcendence." And with that side of himself which never ceases to combat all kinds of naturalism, he combats this philosophy of his own with the rest. To go into this fully would involve a detailed analysis of Croce's other works, and we shall not pursue it here. But we must refer to it, and insist upon this general principle: that there are two Croces, the realist, dualist, empiricist, or naturalist, who delights in formal distinctions and habitually works in dualistic or transcendent terms, and the idealist, whose whole life is a warfare upon transcendence and naturalism in all their forms, who sweeps away dualisms and reunites distinctions in a concrete or immanent unity. A great part of Croce's written work consists in a debate between these two, one building up dualisms and the other dismantling them; sometimes failing to dismantle them. This we shall find throughout the present book. In fact, at the end of our inquiry, we shall see reason to suspect that this double-mindedness has now become so intolerable to Croce himself that he feels impelled to destroy altogether a philosophy so deeply at variance with itself, and to take refuge in a new field of activity.

The dualism between history and annals is really, if I understand it aright, an expository or "pedagogic" dualism, confused by the attempt to interpret it as a real or philosophical dualism, to which end it has been mistakenly identified with the distinction between a symbol and its meaning. An expository dualism is a common enough device: in order to expound a new idea one frequently distinguishes it point by point from an old, thereby developing what looks like a dualism between them, without, however, at all meaning to imply that the dualism is real, and that the old conception has a permanent place in one's philosophy alongside of the new. Thus the antithesis between the flesh and the spirit, developed in order to define the term spirit, is misunderstood if it is hardened into a metaphysical dualism: so again that between mind and matter, art and nature, and so forth. In such cases the two terms are not names for two co-ordinate realities, but an old and a new name for the same thing, or even an old and a new "definition of the Absolute," and the new supersedes the old: if the old is compelled to live on alongside the new, it sets up a dualism whose effect is precisely to destroy the whole meaning of the new conception and to characterise the whole view as a naturalistic or transcendent philosophy.

This is curiously illustrated by Croce's chapter on "History and Annals." "History is living history, annals are dead history: history is contemporary history, annals are past history: history is primarily an act of thought, annals an act of will" (p. 10). Here again the word *primarily* gives everything away; but, ignoring that, it is strange that the category in which annals fall is indifferently, and as it were synonymously, called *the past, dead,* and *the will*. Here—and numerous other passages could be quoted which prove the same thing—Croce is really identifying the distinction of thought and will with the distinction of living and dead, spirit and matter. The will is thought of as the nonspiritual; that is to say, the concept of dead matter has reappeared in the heart of idealism, christened by the strange name of will. This name is given to it because, while Croce holds the idealistic theory that thought thinks itself, he unconsciously holds the realistic or transcendent theory that the will wills not itself but the existence of a lifeless object other than itself, something unspiritual held in existence by an act of the will. Thus, wherever Croce appeals from the concept of thought to the concept of will, he is laying aside his idealism and falling back into a transcendent naturalism.

But now the idealist reasserts himself. A corpse, after all, is not merely dead: it is the source of new life. So annals are a necessary part of the growth of history: thought, as a philosopher has said, "feeds saprophytically upon its own corpse." Annals are therefore not a mere stupid perversion of history, but are essential to history itself. Annals are a "moment" of history, and so therefore is will of thought, matter of mind, death of life, error of truth. Error is the negative moment of thought, without which the positive or constructive moment, criticism, would have nothing to work upon. Criticism in destroying errors constructs truth. So historical criticism, in absorbing and digesting annals, in showing that they are not history, creates the thought that is history. This is idealism; but it stultifies the original dualism. The distinction between history and annals is now not a distinction between what history is (thought) and what history is not (will), but between one act of thought (history) and another act of thought of the same kind, now superseded and laid aside (annals), between the half-truth of an earlier stage in the process of thought and the fuller truth that succeeds it. This is no dualism, no relation between *A* and *not-A*, and therefore it cannot be symbolized by the naturalistic terminology of thought and will; it is the dialectical relation between two phases of one and the same development, which is throughout a process of both thinking and willing.

The same fundamental vice underlies the very attractive discussion of "pseudo-histories." We all know the historian who mistakes mere accuracy for truth, the "philological" historian; and him who mistakes romance for history, the "poetical" historian; and him who imagines that the aim of history is not to tell the truth but to edify or glorify or instruct, the "pragmatic" historian. And Croce characterises them and discusses their faults in an altogether admirable way. But he wants to prove that he has given us a list of all the possible forms of false history, and this can be done by appealing to the list of the "forms of the spirit." But the appeal not only fails in detail—for his list of pseudo-histories tallies very ill with the list of forms of the spirit—but is false in principle.

For "poetical" history, to take an example, is only a name calling attention to a necessary feature of all history. Croce shows how Herodotus, Livy, Tacitus, Grote, Mommsen, Thierry, and so forth, all wrote from a subjective point of view, wrote so that their personal ideals and feelings coloured their whole work and in parts falsified it. Now, if this is so, who wrote real history, history not coloured by points of view and ideals? Clearly, no one. It is not even desirable that anyone should. History, to be, must be seen, and must be seen by somebody, from somebody's point of view. And doubtless, every history so seen will be in part seen falsely. But this is not an accusation against any particular school of historians; it is a law of our nature. The only safe way of avoiding error is to give up looking for the truth.

And here, curiously, Croce breaks out into a panegyric on error, as if conscious that he was being too hard on it. The passage is a most interesting combination of naturalism and idealism. Error, says Croce, is not a "fact"; it is a "spirit"; it is "not a Caliban, but an Ariel, breathing, calling, and enticing from every side, and never by any effort to be solidified into hard fact." This image implies that error does not, as such, exist; that is, that no judgment is wholly or simply erroneous, wholly devoid of truth: which is orthodox idealism, but quite contrary to Croce's general theory of error. But it also implies that error as such is valuable and good: he speaks definitely of the "salutary efficacy of error"; and this conflicts not only with the description of pseudo-histories as "pathological"—and therefore, presumably, to be wholly avoided—but also with Croce's own idealism, and with the view which surely seems reasonable, that the indubitable value and efficacy of errors belongs to them not qua errors but qua (at least partial) truths. An error like historical materialism is, as Croce says, not a fact; that is because, its falsity discovered, it is banished, it becomes a memory. Also, as Croce says, it is, or rather we should say was, useful: it superseded a worse error, historical romanticism. But it was once a fact, and then it was a truth—the best truth that could be had then, anyhow; and then, too, it was useful, as an improvement on its predecessor. To-day it is not a fact (except for historians of thought), nor true, nor yet useful. The passage is confused because Croce is assigning to error as such the merits of truth; which is an attempt to express the fact that error as such does not exist, and that what we call an error is in part true and therefore has the "salutary efficacy" which belongs to truth alone. This confusion is due to the vacillation between naturalism, for which some statements are just true and others just false, and idealism, for which truth and falsehood are inextricably united in every judgment, in so far as it creates itself by criticising another, and becomes itself in turn the object of further criticism.

This vacillation is the more interesting as much of Croce's treatment of error is purely naturalistic, and shows no trace of idealism. His general theory of error, in the *Logica,* is absolutely naturalistic. Thought, he there argues, is as such true, and can never be erroneous: an error, whatever it is, cannot be a thought. What is it, then? Why, an act of will. We need hardly point out the absurdities of such a theory. We only wish to point out its naturalistic character; to lay stress on the distinction implied between a truth, as containing no error, and an error, as containing no truth, correlative with that between pure thinking and pure willing, and based on the same naturalistic or transcendent logic. So again his inquiry into the varieties (phenomenology) of error, in this book and elsewhere, and the list of pseudo-histories, are purely naturalistic; and so again is a highly "transcendent" type of argument not uncommon with him, which traces the origin of a philosophical error to the baneful influence of some other activity of the spirit. Thus philosophical errors, which by their very nature can only have arisen within philosophy itself, are ascribed to science (p. 45, the fallacy of the independent object) and re-

ligion (p. 51, the dualism of *a priori* and *a posteriori* truths),
errors whose only connection with science or religion is that when
philosophers believed in them they applied them to the interpretation of these activities: whereupon Croce, having rejected them
as general philosophical principles, uncritically retains them as
adequate accounts of activities to which he has not paid special attention, and thus credits these activities with originating them.
The result is a kind of mythology, in which Philosophy or
Thought takes the part of a blameless and innocent heroine led
into errors by the villains Science and Religion. These flights of
pure naturalism in Croce have a curious eighteenth-century fla-
vour; it is difficult in reading them to feel ourselves in the fore-
front of modern philosophy; for Science and Religion, the villains
of the piece, represent precisely that Caliban of embodied factual
error whose banishment from philosophy has just been ratified by
Croce himself.

The same naturalism colours the chapter on the "Positivity of
History." Here the doctrine is expounded that "history always
justifies, never condemns." History always expresses positive
judgments, never negative; that is, it explains why things happened as they did, and this is to prove that they happened rightly.
"A fact which seems merely bad is a non-historical fact," a fact
not yet thought out successfully by the historian, not yet understood. The historian as such therefore always justifies: if he condemns, he proves himself no historian. What is he, then? Why, a
partisan; one who acts instead of thinking, serves practical instead
of theoretical needs. The historian as such is a thinker; "the history which once was lived is by him thought, and in thought the
antitheses which arose in volition or feeling no longer exist." To
condemn in thought is to "confuse thought with life."

Here as usual we sympathise warmly: we know the historian
who regards history as a melodrama, and we do not regard him
as the best kind of historian. But we are trying at present to think
philosophically; and the dualism between thought and life makes

us a little uncomfortable. Life, we are told, is the scene of value-judgments, judgments of good and evil, which are products of the will; thought knows only the truth, and in the eye of thought everything that is, is justified. Partiality is proper and necessary to action, impartiality to thought. The statesman calls his opponent wicked or misguided, because, being a man of action and not a man of thought, it is not his business to understand him, but only to defeat him; the historian, understanding the motives of both, calls both alike wise and good.

This is the same tangled skein of idealism and naturalism. The underlying truth, that no historical event, no act and no person, is merely evil, and that it is the duty of the historian to discover and express the good which our hastier analysis of the facts has failed to reveal—this is an important doctrine, and it is an ideal-istic one; but the terms in which Croce has stated it are naturalistic. The distinction between theoretical and practical men, activities, or points of view is pure naturalism, and here it leads Croce into plain and obvious misstatements. It is monstrous to say that par-tiality is right and necessary in a statesman and wrong in a his-torian. Each alike ought to be as impartial as he possibly can in the process of balancing claims and forming a judgment on them; and each must be partial in asserting his judgment, when he has formed it, against his opponent's. The statesman ought to show all the impartiality he can in judging the claims of capital and labour, or agriculture and industry, however energetically he sup-ports his own bills and denounces those of his opponents; and if the historian is impartial in balancing evidence and understand-ing motives, we do not expect him to be so impartial as to declare a rival's view of the character of Richard III as good as his own. Because thought must be impartial, are there to be no more con-troversies?

Controversies, yes, it may be said, but not condemnations. We may refute Mommsen, but we must not condemn Julius Caesar. But this is quite unreasonable. If I may think a German professor wrong, why not a Roman general? If, as an historian of warfare, I must accept all Caesar's battles as impeccable, then as an historian of the history of warfare I must accept all Mommsen's accounts of them as impeccable for the same reason. Controversy is for contemporaries, no doubt: *de mortuis nil nisi bonum.* But as Caesar's historian I am—is not Croce forgetting it?—Caesar's contemporary. When a man is dead, the world has judged him, and my judgment does not matter; but the mere fact that I am rethinking his history proves that he is not dead, that the world has not yet passed its judgment. In my person, indeed, it is now about to pass judgment. Croce's contention is that I am forbidden to pass any but an exclusively favourable judgment. Why is this? It is because Croce is here assuming a "transcendent" theory of knowledge, according to which judgment has already been passed in a court outside the mind of the historian, a court from which he has no appeal. He can only write down what he finds written on the page of History.

Thus the idealistic principle that there is a positive side in every historical fact is combined with the naturalistic assumption that the positive side excludes a negative side; the principle that nothing is merely bad is misunderstood as implying that everything is wholly good, and not bad in any sense at all. And this naturalistic misinterpretation of an idealistic principle confuses the whole argument to such an extent that it actually necessitates a naturalistic and transcendent theory of knowledge. Only in the light of such a theory can it be maintained, as Croce here maintains, that every historical event is right, and therefore everyone who thinks otherwise is wrong, as if the opinions of these poor creatures were not also historical events.

The dualism of thought and life is thus pure transcendence, a formal contradiction of Croce's own theory of history. Thought is life, and therefore the historian can never be impartial; he can only struggle to overcome one prejudice after another, and trust to his successors to carry on the work. The progress of thought is always negative in that it means a continual controversy with one-self and within oneself. The abstract "positivity of history" is a delusion, bred of a naturalistic philosophy.

In the same spirit Croce proceeds to expound his conception of progress. There being no negativity in history, that is to say, none in the world of reality, all is progress, every change is, as he says, "a change from the good to the better." There is no such thing as decadence; what appears to be so is really progress, if only you look at it from the right point of view. True; there always is such a point of view, and it is of the utmost importance that we should not overlook it. But there is the opposite point of view too. A change that is really a progress seen from one end is no less really a decadence, seen from the other. It is true to say that the decay of archery was the rise of firearms; but it is not less true to say that the rise of firearms was the decay of archery. Here is one point of view against another: which is the right one? Croce an-swers emphatically that one is altogether right and the other alto-gether wrong. But why? Is it the historian's duty always to take the side of the big battalions just because they win? Is he always to side with the gods against Cato? Or do we not rather feel that it was just by siding against Cato that the gods proved themselves no true gods? The historian's duty is surely not to pick and choose: he must make every point of view his own, and not condemn the lost cause merely because it is lost. The fact is that Croce is here again taking a transcendent attitude, asserting the existence of a criterion outside the historian's mind by which the points of view which arise within that mind are justified and condemned.

It is the less surprising to find this transcendence emerge into full daylight at the end of the chapter. Croce is saying that when a historian fails to maintain a properly "positive" attitude, fails, that is, to maintain that whatever happens is right, he does so be-cause he has attached himself so blindly to a cause, a person, an institution, a truth, as to forget that every individual thing is but mortal; and when his foolish hopes are shattered and the beloved object dies in his arms, the face of the world is darkened and he can see nothing in the change but the destruction of that which he loved, and can only repeat the sad story of its death. "All histories which tell of the decay and death of peoples and institutions are false"; "elegiac history" is always partisan history. This he expands by saying that immortality is the prerogative of the spirit in general: the spirit in its determinate and particular forms always perishes and always must perish.

Here the transcendence is explicit and unequivocal. The "spirit in general" is presented as having characters (immortality, absoluteness) which the individual spirit has not; the whole is the negation of the part; the absolute or infinite is something over against, contrasted with, the finite. The Christianity at which Croce never ceases to gird for its transcendence is here, as often, immanent exactly where he is himself transcendent. It knows that life is reached through death and found in death, and that to live without dying is to die indeed.

The whole discussion of the "positivity of history" is, in fact, vitiated by naturalism. The truth which Croce wishes to express is the same which Hegel concealed beneath his famous phrase, "the real is the rational." What happens, happens for a good reason, and it is the business of history to trace the reason and state it. And that means to justify the event. But this truth is grossly distorted if it is twisted into the service of a vulgar optimism which takes it for the whole truth. Hegel's view of reality, as Croce himself has insisted, was no such vulgar optimism, but a tragic view; and yet the common charge of optimism brought against him is not unfounded, for he, like Croce, had in him a streak of naturalism which at last overcame him. The point of view here maintained by Croce, from which every change is for the better, and all partisans of lost causes are fools and blasphemers, is neither better nor worse in itself than that from which all change is for the worse, and all innovators are Bolsheviks and scoundrels. A history which was merely a tragedy or a series of

tragedies, like the "Monk's Tale" in Chaucer, would be a mis-
representation of reality; but to hold that all tragedy is delusion
and error, and that reality contains no tragic elements at all, is to
misrepresent it no less gravely. To imagine that the choice lies between these two misrepresentations, that a positive and a negative
moment cannot coexist in reality, is just the kind of error that
characterises a transcendent or naturalistic philosophy.

We are now in a position to consider the relation between history, science, and philosophy. Science Croce identifies with the
generalising activity of the mind. History is the internal and individual understanding of an object into which the mind so enters
that subject and object can no longer be separated; it is real thinking. Science is the external and arbitrary construction of abstract
types, and the manipulation of them for practical ends; it is not
thinking at all, but willing. This is Croce's distinction. It falls, we
observe, within the competence of Croce the naturalist, appealing
as it does to the abstract scheme of thought and will. What does
Croce the idealist say to it? For it is evident that he cannot assent
to it.

He answers the question tacitly in a chapter on "Natural History." Here he denounces that kind of "history" which proceeds
by making abstract classifications and then spreads out the classes
over a chronological scale; for instance, that kind of history of
language which imagines that language began by being monosyl-
labic, and then went on to polysyllabic forms, or that history of
morals and society which begins with pure egoism and goes on to
"deduce" altruism, and so on. He shows that this type of fallacy,
in which temporal sequence is used as a kind of mythology for
logical or spacial interrelation, is found not only in the sciences
of nature but also in the sciences of man. In both alike, he says,
we classify and arrange our facts, and make abstract generalisations which can, if we like, be arranged along an imaginary time-
scale. But also, in both alike we can do real thinking: we can
enter into the individual and understand it from within. The ob-

ject, whether "a neolithic Ligurian or a blade of grass," can be penetrated by thought and lived by the thinker.

This simply destroys the distinction between science and history. It proves that as science (abstract classification) enters into the work of the historian, so history (concrete individual thought) enters into the work of the scientist. We are generally told that the business of the scientist consists of classifying and abstracting: this, we now see, is not the case. A scientist is intrinsically no more concerned with generalising than an historian. Each does generalise; the geologist generalises about classes of rocks, as the historian generalises about classes of manuscripts; but in each case the generalisation is the means to that thinking which is the man's real work. The historian's real work is the reconstruction in thought of a particular historical event; the geologist's, the reconstruction in thought of a particular geological epoch at a particular place. If the anthropologist's aim is to be a neolithic Ligurian, the botanist's is to be a blade of grass.

Croce does not say this explicitly, but it is all implied in what he does say. He is in the habit of maintaining, formally, the naturalistic distinction of science and history, as concerned with generalisations and individuals respectively; but what he calls science is only one fragment of what he knows history to be, and equally it is only one fragment of what science really is. But, not being perhaps so deeply versed in science as he is in history, he readily misunderstands the true nature of scientific thinking, uncritically swallowing whole the naturalistic logic and mistaking one subordinate aspect of science for the whole.

The relation of philosophy to history is a subject often touched on in this book, but in the end left extremely obscure. The obscurity is due to a vacillation between two views; the idealistic strain of Croce's thought maintaining (with Gentile, to whom this side of Croce seems to be not a little indebted) the identity of philosophy and history, and the naturalistic maintaining that philosophy is a component part of history.

The two views are held side by side, without any attempt at reconciliation: probably without consciousness of the discrepancy. But no one who collects the relevant passages can fail to be struck by the contrast. Thus, on page 17 "philology" (*i.e.*, fact) "combines with philosophy" (*i.e.*, critical thought) "to form history"; on page 71 "philosophy is history and history is philosophy"; on page 136 philosophy is "the methodological moment of history"; and on page 162 "there is no way of distinguishing historical thought from philosophical." The two views seem to alternate with curious regularity.

The view that history and philosophy are identical is derived from reflections like those with which this paper began. Each without the other is a lifeless corpse: every piece of real thinking is both at once. This is Gentile's view. But the view that philosophy is a mere subordinate moment in history has quite different motives. It seems to indicate that historical thought is conceived as real or absolute thought, containing philosophy complete within itself; while philosophy by itself is an inferior form, abstract and at best only half true, which requires to be supplemented by "philology" or the study of fact, and so converted into the perfect form of history. We are reminded of Vico's alliance between philosophy and philology by the language here, and of Hegel's dialectic by the thought that one form of activity is inherently imperfect and requires to be transformed into another before it can be satisfactory.

It is to this latter view that Croce seems finally to incline. In an appendix written some years after the body of the book he states it definitely: philosophy is the "methodological moment of history," that is, the working-out and critical construction of the concepts which history employs in its work. And this is an immanent methodology—it goes on not outside history, in a separate laboratory, but within the process of historical thinking itself. The philosopher and the historian have returned from the ride, in fact, with the philosopher inside.

CROCE'S PHILOSOPHY OF HISTORY 21

This seems to me to indicate two things: the triumph within philosophy of Croce the naturalist over Croce the idealist, and the shifting of Croce's own centre of interest from philosophy to history.

The naturalist triumphs over the idealist because the synthesis of philosophy and philology in history implies the naturalistic conception of philosophy and philology as two different and anti-thetical forms of activity, which again implies that ideas or categories, or whatever is the subject-matter of philosophy, are something different from facts, the subject-matter of philology. Such a dualism of idea and fact is wholly impossible to an idealist; and yet only on this assumption can it be maintained that philosophy is immanent in history while history is transcendent with reference to philosophy. Naturalism, transcendence, is the last word.

Further, Croce here shows, if I read his meaning aright, that he is gradually deserting philosophy for history. He appears to have come to the conclusion that philosophical truth is to be attained not by direct fire—by the study of philosophy in the ordinary sense, which he now pronounces a delusion—but indirectly, as a product of ordinary historical work. Philosophy in his mind is being absorbed in history; the two are not poised in equilibrium, as with Gentile, but one is cancelled out entirely as already provided for by the other. This is made clear by the appendix on "Philosophy and Methodology," which consists of an enumeration of the advantages which he hopes to gain from the new concept of philosophy—solid advantages for the most part, from which philosophy will be the gainer, but all, as he states them, tinged with a very visible weariness of philosophical work.

If this is really the case, and if Croce gives up philosophy to devote himself to history and to the reform of Italian education, it is not for us to repine. It is impossible not to observe in this book (and one sees the same thing in his other books) how his philosophy improves when he turns to handle the more strictly historical problems: how such a sophism as that concerning the "positivity of history" is calmly ignored, or rather the underlying truth of it unerringly seized upon, when he comes to assign their value to the various historical periods, and how the naturalistic element in his thought purges itself away when he becomes an historian, leaving an atmosphere of pure idealism. To say that Croce is a better historian than philosopher would be a misstatement of the truth, which is rather that the idealistic philosophy at which he has always consistently aimed is unable to penetrate the naturalistic framework to which, as a philosopher, he seems to have irreparably committed himself, and is only free to develop fully when he shakes off the associations of technical philosophy and embarks on work of a different kind. The necessity for this change of occupation he is tempted to ascribe to something in the very nature of philosophy and history; but this is an illusion, itself part of the very naturalism from which he is trying to escape. The real necessity for it lies in himself alone, in his failure to purge his philosophy of its naturalistic elements.

If this is so, Croce's desertion of philosophy for history may be only an unconscious step forward in philosophy: a kind of philosophical suicide by which, casting off the abstract "philosophy of the spirit," which by now has become intolerable even to himself, he can reach the point of absolute idealism to which his successors Gentile and De Ruggiero have already carried his thought.

Are History and Science Different Kinds of Knowledge?*

F ROM THE POINT OF VIEW of the theory of knowledge or
logic, must a distinction be drawn between two kinds of
knowledge called respectively History and Science?

Such a distinction is usually made: we shall argue that it is
illusory. It is implicit[1] in the whole drift of the Platonic philosophy, though Plato nowhere, I think, states it clearly. But Aristotle not only states it, but states it in a way which, though only
incidental, implies that it is familiar. In a well-known passage
of the *Poetics* he remarks that poetry is more scientific[2] than history, because poetry deals with the universal, for instance, what
a generalised type of man would do on a generalised type of

---

* Reprinted from *Mind* (1922), with the permission of the editor.

[1] I would suggest, for instance, that just so far as Mr. H. J. Paton
(*Proc. Arist. Soc.* [1922], pp. 69 *seqq.*) is right in identifying εἰκασία in
Plato with art, so far πίστις is to be identified with history, as cognition
of the actual, but only γιγνόμενον, individual.

[2] φιλοσοφώτερον. I need hardly remind the reader that what we call
science Aristotle regularly calls φιλοσοφία, a usage long followed in this
country and criticised rather spitefully by Hegel. What we nowadays
(having given in to Hegel) call philosophy Aristotle calls σοφία,
θεολογία, or πρώτη φιλοσοφία.

occasion (and this, he implies, as *knowledge of the universal,* is science), whereas history deals with particular facts such as what, on a particular occasion, a particular person said. History is thus the *knowledge of the particular.*

I. The distinction between history as knowledge of the particular and science as knowledge of the universal has become common property and is in general accepted without question. We propose to criticise it: and as a preliminary, we shall indicate two difficulties which we shall not follow up.

(*a*) It implies a metaphysical distinction between two kinds of entity, a *particular* and a *universal,* such that any cognition may be knowledge of the one in isolation from the other. This dualism is precisely the doctrine which Plato attacked in the *Parmenides* when he pointed out that the universal, thus distinguished from the particular as a separate object, loses just its universality and becomes merely another particular. The mediaeval nominalists attacked it again, in the form in which the realists held it: and Berkeley once more attacked it in the doctrine of abstract ideas. Any one of these three arguments could be directed with disastrous effect on the metaphysical groundwork of the distinction between history and science: but we shall not undertake this task because the arguments in question are purely destructive, and like all destructive arguments would be waved aside as mere examples of the "difficulties" which seem only to stimulate the faith of the believer.

(*b*) We might drop metaphysics and appeal to experience, which clearly enough shows the instability of such a dualism. Wherever people have distinguished science and history as different kinds of knowledge they have tended to degrade one into the position of a pseudo-knowledge and to erect the other into the only real knowledge.

(i) In Greek thought science or knowledge of the universal is real knowledge and history or knowledge of the particular is only half-knowledge. For Plato the particular is midway between being and not-being, and therefore our best possible cognitions of it are midway between knowledge and ignorance. They are not knowledge: they are mere opinion. For Aristotle the qualification of poetry as more scientific than history implies that poetry (and therefore *a fortiori* science) comes nearer to satisfying the ideal of knowledge than history does. This position became traditional, and crops out in a curious way in the nineteenth century. It was common in that period to propose that history should be elevated to the rank of a science: which meant that it had hitherto not been a science because it only recognised the particular, but that now this reproach was to be removed, and after a long apprenticeship spent in the proper Baconian way in collecting facts history was to be promoted to the task of framing general laws, and thereby converted into a science fit to take its place among the other sciences like chemistry and mechanics. This proposal, to redeem history from its degraded infra-scientific position, became part of the regular programme of nineteenth-century empiricism and positivism, and the science into which it was to be converted was variously entitled Anthropology, Economics, Political or Social Science, the Philosophy of History, and Sociology.

(ii) The opposite tendency has been late in appearing, but it has made amends for its lateness. The chief feature of European philosophy in the last generation has been that movement of reaction from nineteenth-century positivism which has tended to degrade science into a false form of knowledge and to find the true form in history. The metaphysical notion of reality as process, movement, change, or becoming has had its reverse (perhaps really its obverse) side in an epistemology which places history at the centre of knowledge. In this, implicitly if not explicitly, the schools of Mach, of Bergson, of James, and of Croce agree: and even more plainly they agree in holding that science is not knowledge at all but action, not true but useful, an object of discussion not to epistemology but to ethics. Any cognition (such seems to be the Berkeleian principle common to these schools) must be of the particular, and must therefore be history: what is called a cognition of the universal cannot be a cognition at all but must be an action. They do not all intend by this analysis to "degrade" science in the sense of denying its *value*: for it is, they maintain, *useful*: what they deny is simply its truth.

Experience shows the difficulty of keeping the balance even and the temptation to identify the genus knowledge with one of its species, thereby reducing the other to the position of an expedient towards knowledge or an inferior kind of knowledge. But no one who really wishes to maintain the dualism will let this deter him. Grant that every one from Plato to Croce has failed to maintain it, *he* will not fail but will stand by the very simple doctrine that knowledge is a genus with two species: knowledge of the particular, history, and knowledge of the universal, science. This simple faith in the possibility of maintaining a dualism by sheer will-power, undeterred by the spectacle of the bleaching bones of previous adventures, is left untouched by the expressions of a disillusioned scepticism. We shall not pursue this line of criticism, but shall try simply to describe how the scientist and the historian work, in order to see whether we can detect a fundamental difference between them.

II. It is commonly assumed that what the scientist does, in virtue of which he is a scientist, is to generalise. Everything else which he may do, it is thought, is (in so far as he is a scientist) a means to this end. When it is achieved his work is done and there is nothing more for him to do except to go on and frame a new generalisation. That is the meaning of the common saying that science is the knowledge of the universal. Is it true?

As a common opinion it may be countered with another. Generalisations can be learnt by hearsay or reading: for instance, you may learn by heart the list of fossils characteristic of a certain horizon by simply getting them up from a book. Now common opinion holds that a man may be book-learned in a science and yet incompetent in it. A geologist may know the names of fossils, but if we find on putting him down in front of an actual landscape or in an actual quarry that he cannot give us a geological account of this particular object, we say that he is an imposter. He can repeat, it may be, all the generalisations which (we generally think) constitute the *corpus* of geological science, but if he cannot apply them he is no geologist.

Friends and enemies of the natural sciences agree in thinking the *application* of generalisations to be characteristic of them, and so it is, but not in quite the way that is generally thought. "Science" is praised or despised for its practical or economic value, and the geologist is respected or scorned for being able to tell us where to look for coal. It is implied that geology means not merely knowing generalities but interpreting particular facts in the light of these generalities: being able to say "my geological learning leads me to believe that there is coal just below this sandstone." And it is implied that the person who says this is more entitled to the name of geologist than one who just reels off general statements.

The common view of science as essentially useful or utilitarian is not wholly erroneous; it conceals an important truth, namely that a scientist is only a scientist ἐνεργεία when he is interpreting concrete facts in the light of his general concepts, and that the framing of these concepts, if regarded as something distinct from the application of them, is not the end of science but the means. The geologist ἐνεργεία is the man who is occupied not in repeating, nor even in inferring, generalised truths, but in looking at country with a geologist's eye, understanding it geologically as he looks at it, or "applying" his geological concepts to the interpretation of what he sees. To possess these concepts without so applying them is not (as the view which identifies science with generalisation would imply) to be an actual geologist, but only at most to be a potential geologist, to possess the tools of a geologist without using them. But we are here in danger of a serious mistake. The potential geologist is only a mythological abstraction: he cannot really exist: for where the "tool" is a concept and the "use" of it is the interpretation of individual fact by its means, the tool cannot be possessed in idleness. That would be to strain the metaphor. Interpretation is not the employment of a previously-constructed tool (concept) upon a separately-given material (fact) : neither the concept nor the fact is "possessed" (*thought* and *observed* respectively) except in the presence of the other. To possess or think a concept is to interpret a fact in terms of it: to possess or observe a fact is to interpret it in terms of a concept.

Science is this interpretation. To live the life of a scientist consists in the understanding of the world around one in terms of one's science. To be a geologist is to look at landscape geologically: to be a physiologist is to look at organisms physiologically, and so on. The object which the scientist cognises is not "a universal," but always particular fact, a fact which but for the existence of his generalising activity would be blank meaningless sense-data. His activity as a scientist may be described alternatively as the *understanding* of sense-data by concepts, or the *realising* of concepts in sensation, "intuiting" his thoughts or "thinking out" his intuitions. In this process he recognises the objects before him as being of this or that kind: and sometimes this recognition results in the discovery that they are economically valuable, that is, it serves as a basis for action. That is the truth which underlies the idea of science as essentially utilitarian: but if we are to use technicalities we shall say that utility is not its *essence* but its *accident*, or at most its *property*, since ability to use one's world perhaps follows necessarily from understanding it. And every science has the same character: not only geology and physiology but even what we are accustomed to consider the most abstract sciences. Thus, to be a chemist consists not in knowing general formulae but in interpreting particular changes which we observe taking place by means of these formulae: the science of mechanics consists in the similar interpretation of observed motions: even mathematics does not consist of abstract equations and formulae but in the application of these to the interpretation of our own mathematical operations.

A distinction is often made between the particular and the individual, the former as a mere abstraction, the latter as the concrete fact, synthesis of two opposite abstractions, the particular and the universal. If we must conform to this usage we shall put our contention by saying that there is no such thing as knowledge either of the particular or of the universal, but only of the individual: and that the sense-datum (pure particular) and concept (pure universal) are false abstractions when taken separately which yet, as elements in the one concrete object of knowledge, the individual interpreted fact, are capable of being analytically distinguished. This may be illustrated by the fallacy of inductive logic. The inductive logician assumes that the task of science is to generalise, to frame universal laws; and that its starting-point is the facts of ordinary observation. The problem of inductive logic then is how, from the particular facts, do we reach the universal law? It tries to describe this process in detail: but when it has done so one cannot help seeing that the alleged particular from which it started was never a pure particular but was already steeped in generality. The process ought to have begun with the pure uninterpreted sense-datum. It never does so begin in the descriptions of inductive logicians, for two excellent reasons: such a pure sense-datum does not exist except as an abstraction and therefore cannot be the concrete starting-point of a process, and if it did exist one could never get beyond it to reach the universal. So the inductive logician makes the process begin with the carefully staged experiment or intelligently recorded observation, which is not a *particular* at all but an *indi-*

vidual, a concrete fact bristling with conceptual interpretations; and from this point, which already contains and presupposes the concept, he proceeds to "induce" the concept he has surreptitiously presupposed. How, after this, he has the face to accuse syllogistic logic of *petitio principii* remains a mystery.

The scientist's aim is, then, not to "know the universal" but to know the individual, to interpret intuitions by concepts or to realise concepts in intuitions. The reason why it has so often been fancied that his aim is to form generalisations is probably that we expect science to be contained in textbooks, much as we expect art to be contained in pictures. Art is to be found not in pictures but in our activity which has pictures for its object: and science is to be found in our activity which uses scientific textbooks, not in the textbooks themselves. The teacher who puts a textbook into the hands of a student must be understood as saying: "I give you not science, but the key to science: the information here printed is not science, it is something which when you find out how to use it will help you to build up in your own mind an activity which alone is itself science." It is only because this is so obvious and so continually goes without saying that we habitually overlook it.

III. The scientist generalises, certainly: but generalisation is subordinate to his real work as a scientist, the interpretation of individual fact. But the historian does not remain at a level of thought below generalisation: he generalises too and with exactly the same kind of purpose. Such generalisations as charters, mediaeval scripts, types of handwriting characteristic of the early fourteenth century, guild institutions, and so forth, go to the interpretation of a scrap of parchment which fits into its place as a link in the history of a town precisely as fossils, Jurassic fauna, shells peculiar to the Portland beds, and so on, are the concepts through which a geologist works out the geological history of a valley. Of late, the historian's concepts have tended increasingly to group themselves into what seem to be independent sciences, palaeography, numismatics, archaeology and so forth. If, as is mostly the case, they do their work better for being thus incorporated into chartered societies, well and good. But their work is the interpretation of individual fact, the reconstruction of historical narrative: and there is a certain danger that the archaeologist, under the influence of the false theory of science which we have criticised, may forget this. He may even think that poor old history has been quite superseded by his own science and others like it, whose aim is not to individualise but to generalise: to reach conclusions not in the form "we can now assert that Agricola built this fort" but in the form "we can now assert that Samian bowls of shape 29 went out of use about A.D. 80." The latter is certainly the form in which the conclusions of many valuable monographs appear: but that is just because the monograph as a whole is only an incident in the scientific lives of its writer and readers, an incident whose importance lies in its bearing on the interpretation of individual facts. Monographs are not archaeology: or if they are, then archaeology is a false abstraction and we must say monographs are not history, since history is the concrete activity which produces and uses them.

The nineteenth-century positivists were right in thinking that history could and would become more scientific. It did, partly as a result of their work, become at once more critical and trustworthy, and also more interested in general concepts. But its interest in general concepts, reflected in the rise of archaeology and such sciences, was the interest of a workman in the improvement of his tools. History did not subordinate the determination of facts to the framing of general laws based on them; that idea was part and parcel of the inductive fallacy. It created within itself new bodies of generalised thought subordinated to its own supreme end, the determination or interpretation of individual fact.

IV. The analysis of science in epistemological terms is thus identical with the analysis of history, and the distinction between them as separate kinds of knowledge is an illusion. The reason for this illusion is to be sought in the history of thought. The ancients developed a very much higher type of scientific than of historical thought: such sciences as mathematics, physics, logic, astronomy, etc., in the hands of the Greeks attained a pitch of excellence which history did not rival till the seventeenth century. Their philosophical reflexions were therefore concentrated on scientific thought and not on the less remarkable achievements of history: and from that time till the nineteenth century a lack of balance between the epistemology of science and that of history continued to exist. The result was that in the theory of science attention has always been drawn to the concepts of principles of interpretation according to which the active work of thought proceeds, while the theory of history has contented itself with attending to the finished product of thought, the fully-compiled historical narrative. This is the root of all the alleged differences between history and science. Thus it has been said that science predicts, whereas history only records the past. That is untrue (geology records the past, history predicts that green-glaze pottery will be found in a mediaeval ruin) except in the sense that what we arbitrarily call history—the finished narrative when the historian has stopped working on it—is complete and immovable, while what we arbitrarily call science (the mere abstract generalisation) is an early stage in the process of thought which looks forward to its own completion in what inductive logic calls verification.

Again, it is said that the mainspring of science is critical thought, that of history authority. That again is wholly untrue unless we are speaking of *incipient* science and *completed* history: for every kind of work is critical so long as the conclusion is not yet reached, and every kind dogmatic when it is. A working historian is critical in all the same ways as a working scientist, and a scientist who has come to a conclusion states it, everybody knows, as dogmatically as a Pope: it would be a pedantic and insincere affectation if he did not.

These and other fancied distinctions are the result of comparing an inside view of science with an outside view of history—science as an actual process of thought with history as a dead, finished article. When both are regarded as actual inquiries, the difference of method and of logic wholly disappears. The traditional distinction, we have suggested, has its origin in a simple historical fact, the fact that science became an object of philosophical reflexion long before history: not in any epistemological dualism. To erect such a dualism is to falsify both science and history by mutilating each of one essential element of knowledge—the element of generalisation or the element of individualisation: and so mutilated, it is not surprising if now history, now science, should appear an illegitimate form of knowledge.

The Nature and Aims of a Philosophy of History*

I. WHAT THE PHILOSOPHY OF HISTORY IS NOT.

THERE ARE TWO INQUIRIES which, for various reasons, have claimed the title of philosophy of history, and have, as I hope to show, claimed it illegitimately. First, the attempt has been made to discover general laws which govern the course of history: laws concerning the successive forms assumed by constitutions; the alternation of high and low, or advancing and declining, civilisations; the implications of a special degree of excellence in art, in religion, in warfare, in commerce; and so forth. These laws are conceived naturalistically; that is to say, as eternal and unchanging truths of which the various events recorded in history are instances; and their discovery is said to be the task of the philosophy of history.

Secondly, the attempt has been made to discover in history not so much an exemplification of eternal abstract laws as the progressive working-out of a single concrete plan; a plan in which every historical incident has a unique place and fulfils a unique purpose, instead of being merely one of an indefinite number of cases in which a law has been exemplified. The philosophy of

* Reprinted from *Proceedings of the Aristotelian Society* (1924–1925), with the permission of the editor.

history, from this point of view, is regarded as the attempt to discover in history some such plan, to trace its development, and to show how the various phases of historical change, as known to us, have tended towards its realisation: to see history as the unfolding of a cosmic drama.

(a) The first of these undertakings aims at the erection of a superstructure of generalisations based upon historical facts. It assumes that the facts have been finally settled by historians; and using these facts as material for inductions, it proceeds to determine the abstract and universal laws which govern their occurrence.

Now this conception is based upon a reality which we shall discuss below; but as it stands it is entirely illusory. First, it is based on a false assumption; the alleged facts upon which it builds its inductions are actually never secure enough to bear the weight that is put upon them, because there is no given fact upon which at any given moment historical research has said the last word, and it is just those "facts" which are most valuable to this kind of philosophy that are most open to question. Secondly, its conclusions are not abstract universal laws, because they are statements about a contingent and transitory subject-matter; generalisations which pretend to be true of all history are, as a matter of fact, true only of certain phases in history. And, thirdly, it ignores just that which most fundamentally characterises history, namely, its individuality; it treats, as if they were mere recurring instances of a principle, facts which are in reality unique. In all these three ways it shows the most radical misunderstanding of history that could possibly be imagined.

But it is based upon a reality; and this reality is the fact that within the body of historical thought itself, not erected upon it as a superstructure but contained within itself as a subordinate but necessary element, generalisation and inductive thinking have an important place. Historical research cannot proceed without using its own previous results as materials upon which to gen-

eralise in order thereby to help itself in the determination of
fresh facts. Actual historical thinking is a constant alternation
of the general and the individual, the individual as end and the
general as means. No historical fact can be determined without
the help of generalisations; thus it is only through inductive
study of ancient pottery that a man can recognise the presence of
a Roman villa in his garden. This inductive study is itself based
on ascertained facts; but these facts in their turn are never at any
given moment finally ascertained; for instance, the discovery of
this Roman villa may bring into question doctrines hitherto generally accepted as to the provenance and date of some kinds of
pottery. The determination of facts and the using of them as
material for generalisations are not two separate and independent
activities, one history and the other the philosophy of history;
they are two interlocking and interacting elements in history
itself. By adequate attention to its own generalising element history becomes scientific; but by trying to separate the two elements
and giving one to the historian and the other to the scientist we
get a history that is scandalously unscientific and a science (which
may call itself a philosophy if it likes) that is scandalously unhistorical.

(b) In the second sense, the philosophy of history has been
conceived as the deciphering of a plan which is working itself
out in the historical process. We need not take the word plan
literally. To do that would be to assume that someone, presumably God, has, so to speak, written in advance the play which in
the history of the world he is producing. Such a drastic theological determinism is not likely to find supporters to-day, and
therefore it need not be attacked. The plan which is revealed in
history is a plan which does not pre-exist to its own revelation;
history is a drama, but an extemporised drama, co-operatively
extemporised by its own performers.

This is a view of history which I, for one, am prepared to
defend. To deny it would involve asserting that history consists

of an indefinite series of atomic events, each wholly devoid of connexion with those which happen before and after; or an indefinite number of simultaneous series of this kind, if we may nowadays use the word simultaneous. But this is neither more nor less plausible than to assert that *Paradise Lost* consists of a series of words none of which has any connexion with the word before it or the word after it. There might be such a series of words; and the fact that Milton wrote this particular series does not prove that it is not such a series, for Milton might have been a person who spent his time "dabbing" for words in a dictionary and putting them down in that order. The way in which we know that *Paradise Lost* is an organised and coherent whole is by reading it and seeing that it is such a whole; and the way we know that history is an organised and coherent whole is by studying history and seeing the connexions between event and event. There is in history a necessary relation between one event and another; and the more closely one studies any period of history the more clearly one sees it as a whole whose parts mutually condition one another, the antecedents being necessary if the consequents are to exist, and the consequents necessary if the antecedents are to be understood. The period thus reveals itself to the historian as a drama in the sense of an organised and coherent whole of events; and if it is suggested that this is a mere illusion incidental to the historian's point of view, it is at least odd that historians should be, as the suggestion implies, the people who know least about history.

But if the parts have a plot, the whole must have a plot; for the parts are only fragments of the whole, not self-contained entities; and their fragmentariness visibly detracts from, instead of enhancing, the coherence of each. A long period of history hangs together better than a short; and the loose ends which are left in the plot of any given period are knit up in the fabric of its context. History as a whole, if only we could know it as a whole, would certainly reveal itself as infinitely more coherent and systematic, infinitely more pervaded by a plot, than any mere period of history.

But to read this plot is not the philosophy of history. It is simply history. If it is the historian's work to discover the details, it cannot be anybody's work but the historian's to discover the interconnexion of the details. This is true on whatever scale we are working; if it is for the historian to see the plot of the Norman Conquest or the French Revolution, it is equally for the historian to see the plot of all history as known to us. In fact, the history and the plot of the history are not two things but one thing; to know history and to know its plot are the work not of two kinds of men but of one.

On the other hand, when we speak of the plot of a story we sometimes mean not the whole story in all its details but an abstract of the story, in which some incidents are omitted and some retained. Such an abstract is not the story but a mutilated version of the story, and its plot is therefore not the real plot of the story but a mutilated version of the plot. Yet it may be a useful expedient towards the comprehension of the real plot. On first approaching a story one may be unable to see the wood for the trees, one may be at first overwhelmed by that very luxuriance of detail which, when one has mastered it, will prove so illuminating. There are, for instance, novelists whose books are obscure not through any fault of imagination or technique, but just because of their virtues; writers who are "difficult" because they see the significance of details which to a less penetrating eye appear meaningless. The reader, in learning to understand such a writer, is helped by being given a simplified outline of the story; an outline in which everything is omitted except the incidents whose significance he can grasp. With this in his head, he returns to the book and finds that the hitherto unrelated and meaningless details fall into place round the fixed points which his simplified outline has given him, so that the whole thing now becomes coherent. This simplified outline is not the plot, but only a preliminary sketch of the plot; a skeleton, we might say, but that metaphor is inadequate because the bones of a skeleton really support the flesh, whereas there is no distinction in principle between those incidents which are included in the outline and those which are not, except that the person for whom the outline is constructed finds the significance of the one easier to understand than the significance of the other. There is no real distinction of greater and less importance in history; history *hat weder Kern noch Schale*; the "crucial" incidents are only those whose crucial character we happen to be able to see.

The real plot of history, then, is coincident with universal history in all its extent and with all its profusion of detail. Omit any part, truncate the course of history or eviscerate some of its detail, and you mutilate the plot, imparting to it a false emphasis and misrepresenting its general significance. But such mutilations and misrepresentations, which are in practice inevitable, are in theory explained by the limits of the historian's intelligence. The ablest and most accomplished historian is only an historian *in fieri,* a man struggling to become an historian; no one can deserve the monstrous flattery of having it said that he saw life whole. But because every historian is trying to see history as a whole, he must form, from time to time, some view as to the character of its skeleton: some working hypothesis as to the things especially worth noticing, especially crucial in their revelation of the nature of the process in which they occur. In reality, as we have said, history has no skeleton; when we fully understand any historical event, each element in it appears as crucial as the rest; but the optical illusion that it has a skeleton is inevitably generated by our own ignorance.

The idea of a philosophy of history in the sense of a plot or scheme of history as a whole thus turns out to be ambiguous. If the plot is a real and concrete plot, like the plot of a novel, if, that is to say, it is the coherence of all history into a single whole, then this plot is nothing apart from the details in which it is

embodied; the plot and the details coincide, and what was called
the philosophy of history turns out to be simply history. If, on
the other hand, the so-called plot of history is a selection of incidents regarded as peculiarly significant, related to history as the
quotations in the analytical programme are related to a sym-
phony, then it is neither history nor philosophy but an expedient
for assisting the historical studies of a generation labouring under
a particular kind of ignorance. Thus, the Marxian economic
interpretation of history was legitimate and in its day valuable if
it implied no more than an emphasis on the need for studying
economic history; but if it is a "philosophical" doctrine to the
effect that economic facts are the only facts of fundamental importance, and form the *real* skeleton of history, it is simply a
philosophical blunder.

In the two accepted senses of the phrase, philosophy of history thus proves a misnomer. The generalising science of history
is an illusion, except in so far as all history already contains in
itself elements of generalisation as a necessary moment of its own
process. The attempt to extract a plot from the details of history
is an illusion, because the plot and the details coincide, and any
plot obtained by omission of some details and emphasis on others
is precisely not the plot of history but a falsified version of that
plot. But of these two conceptions, though both are false, the
second is an advance on the first. To look for a plot in history
means seeing history in its individuality, seeing every incident in
it as an irreplaceable and unique element in an irreplaceable and
unique whole; whereas looking in history for instances of general
laws means failing to grasp the individuality of history and seeing every incident in it as a mere reduplication of a ready-made
type, and the whole as a chaotic assemblage of such reduplica-
tions. This abstract universality is sometimes imagined to be an
advance on the individuality of history, but the opposite is really
the case, because the individual represents not mere particularity
but the synthesis of universal and particular. In other words, to

see the historical individual as unique and irreplaceable does not exclude seeing it as an instance of a rule: on the contrary, it just consists in seeing it as an instance of a rule and at the same time recognising that it is more than a mere instance. Hence the attempt to lay bare the plot of universal history by leaving out the unimportant parts is a failure indeed, but shows a truer grasp on the meaning of history than the attempt to discover laws which the course of history recurrently exemplifies.

II. WHAT THE PHILOSOPHY OF HISTORY IS.

To all actual historians, the philosophy of history, in either of the two senses examined above, is an object of derision; and I do not think this derision is unjust. If someone who calls himself a philosopher tries to erect inductive generalisations upon a basis of historical facts, the historian will say to him: "The facts upon which you are building are hopelessly insecure. Many of them are matters of debate; many are vouched for only by persons anxious to maintain, or unconsciously influenced by, theories like your own; and in proportion as you restrict your premises to facts well attested and generally admitted, your conclusions pass into truisms." If, on the other hand, the philosopher tries to extract from among historical facts the most important, he will reply, "They may seem the most important to you, but they don't to me: and the reason why you think them so important is only that the others have failed to impress you with the quite equal importance which in reality they possess." Both philosophies, the historian feels, are based on bad history, on misunderstanding the nature and status of what goes by the name of historical fact.

This feeling on the part of historians is fully vindicated by a closer analysis. Both philosophies make a common assumption and draw from it a common inference; and not only is the assumption unsound but the inference does not follow from it. The assumption is that there exists a body of wholly ascertained histori-

cal fact which they can use as material; the inference is that therefore they can construct something out of this material which will
throw new light on the nature of the historical facts.

To take the inference first: if the aim of historical thinking is
to ascertain historical facts, then everything that can be said about
those facts, as facts, falls within the scope of historical inquiry;
for until everything that can legitimately be said about them has
been said, they are not wholly ascertained. Every question about
an historical fact is by definition an historical question. Therefore
if a fact has been wholly ascertained, if the historian has finished
with it, nothing more can be said about it. Hence the philosophy
of history has nothing to do; it can, *ex vi terminorum,* throw no
new light on the facts; and it must confine itself to mutilating
them or playing with them. And indeed, of the two philosophies
of history we have criticised, one does nothing except shuffle the
facts, the other does nothing except mutilate them.

But what of the assumption? Is it true that there is in existence
a body of wholly ascertained historical fact? It might appear that
there was; for instance, it is not likely to be questioned that the
battle of Hastings was fought in 1066. But if this fact is said to
be ascertained, what is the fact? What, in other words, is or was
the event whose name is the battle of Hastings? The question
may refer to the tactics of the battle, or to its political significance, to go no further. Now on both these heads we know
something; but no one supposes that we know all that there is to
know. In other words, when we speak of the battle of Hastings
we are speaking not of something known but of something partly
known and partly unknown; and the confidence with which we
speak of it is like the confidence with which we read a label on a
bottle and say "this is arsenic," without anything like an accurate
knowledge of what arsenic is. Lord Kelvin, to a student who
claimed to know what electricity was, replied, "I wish I did";
and that is what anyone who had closely studied the eleventh

century would say to a person who claimed to know what the battle of Hastings was. In the phrase "the battle of Hastings was fought in 1066," the battle of Hastings is a label for something which, no doubt, did happen in that year; but no one knows, no one ever has known, and no one ever will know what exactly it was that happened. This doctrine is not scepticism; for scepticism implies that no one opinion is preferable to any other; and it is certainly possible to choose between different historical views, to show that Freeman's account of the Norman Conquest is defective, for instance, without implying that one knows all there is to be known about it oneself. In other words, no fact ever has been wholly ascertained, but a fact may be progressively ascertained; as the labour of historians goes forward, they come to know more and more about the facts, and to reject with greater and greater confidence a number of mistaken accounts of them; but no historical statement can ever express the complete truth about any single fact.

This is perfectly well known to all historians. No historian imagines that he knows any single fact in its entirety, or that any historian ever will. An historian speaking to historians speaks on the basis of an assumed agreement on this point, and is able to speak as if he thought his own views wholly adequate to the facts: he does not perpetually qualify his statement with "in my opinion," "probably," "so far as the available evidence goes," just because a qualification of this kind is assumed as a standing order in all historical thinking. But the omission of these qualifications lays him open to misunderstanding by anyone who has no experience of historical work and does not know what it is aiming at; and such a person will think that what the historian gives as a probable opinion, based on the available evidence, is a statement of ascertained fact. This is the fundamental error committed by the philosophies of history which we have been examining, and this is why the historian regards them with contempt;

they have got hold of the wrong end of the stick, they show a radical misunderstanding of the very meaning and purpose of historical work.

Ideally, historical thought is the apprehension of a world of fact. Actually, it is the presentation by thought to itself of a world of half-ascertained fact: a world in which truth and error are at any given moment inextricably confused together. Thus the actual object of actual historical thinking is an object which is not "given" but perpetually in process of being given. To philosophise about history as if this object, as it appears at this or that moment, were the reality for which the historian is looking, is to begin at the wrong end. If there is to be a philosophy of history, it can only be a philosophical reflexion on the historian's effort to attain truth, not on a truth which has not been attained.

The philosophy of history, therefore, is the study of historical thinking: not only the psychological analysis of its actual procedure, but the analysis of the ideal which it sets before itself. Historical thought is one among a number of attitudes taken up by the mind towards the objective world; it is an attitude which assumes that there exists a world of facts—not general laws, but individual facts—independent of the being known, and that it is possible, if not wholly to discover these facts, at any rate to discover them in part and approximately. The philosophy of history must be a critical discussion of this attitude, its presuppositions and its implications: an attempt to discover its place in human experience as a whole, its relation to other forms of experience, its origin, and its validity.

Compared with this programme, the philosophies of history which we have hitherto been considering appear as forms of that "dogmatic metaphysics" which Kant believed that he had once for all exploded. They not only assume the validity of historical thought, which the historian himself assumes, but, *plus royalistes que le roi,* they assume that the fruits of this thinking have a certainty and finality which no historian would attribute to them;

and on this basis they try to construct a hybrid view of the objective nature of historical fact which is at once bad history and bad philosophy. Without believing that Kant is the last word in philosophy, one may very well maintain that the attitude which he thought philosophy ought to take up towards natural science is something like the attitude which it ought to take up towards history: not a dogmatic attitude, which swallows whole whatever it thinks—and perhaps wrongly thinks—it has heard historians say, but a critical attitude, which undertakes the task of inquiring not only into the results of a certain type of thought but into the nature and value, the presuppositions and implications, of that type of thought itself.

III. SKETCH OF A PHILOSOPHY OF HISTORY.

The historical consciousness in its ideal nature is the knowledge of the individual. That it aims at being knowledge differentiates it from art, which aims at being imagination: that its object is individual differentiates it from science, which is knowledge of the universal. The object of art is the imaginary individual, whereas the object of history is the real individual. Two artists may present to themselves incompatible objects, without on that account being the worse artists; but if two historians present to themselves incompatible objects (incompatible interpretations, for instance, of the character of Richard III) an error on one side at least is indicated. That is to say, history, like all knowledge, has an object which is one and the same for all knowing minds; namely, the one unique all-inclusive world of historical fact, within which every individual fact has its unique place. Again, as history and art are not identical *a parte objecti,* so history and science are not identical *a parte subjecti.* Both must be called knowledge, because both are amenable to the distinction between truth and falsehood: but scientific thinking is an abstract thinking, historical thinking a concrete thinking. In other words, because the object of science is not a fact but

an abstract type or form, the judgment of science is always
hypothetical: "if *A*, then *B*," where it is not asserted that
A exists in the world of fact. The contact between science and
the world of fact consists in this, that there are in the world
of fact cases very nearly *A*, which are therefore very nearly *B*.
Whereas the object of history is the fact in all its actuality, and
therefore the historical judgment is categorical. No doubt, categorical forms of speech appear in science (all whales are mam-
mals) and hypothetical forms appear in history (if Thucydides
is to be trusted, there was no Pitanate *lochos*). But the former is
not truly categorical, for it does not imply an enumeration of all
actual whales but rather tells us that whatever we can identify as
a whale, if and when we do so identify anything, we can further
identify as a mammal: and the latter is not truly hypothetical, for
the trustworthiness of Thucydides is not the ground of the non-
existence of the Pitanate *lochos*,[1] whereas in a true hypothetical
the antecedent is the ground of the consequent (if equals be
added to equals, the sums are equal). The ideal of history, then,
is to be a single categorical judgment, articulated into an infinity
of coherent categorical judgments, asserting the reality and ex-
pounding the nature of an infinite individual world of fact articulated into an infinity of individual facts. From philosophy, again,
history is differentiated by its objectivity. History assumes that
there is a world of fact independent of the knowing mind, a
world which is only revealed and in no sense constituted by the
historian's thought: it assumes that this thought establishes a
relation of knowledge between two terms, the knowing mind
and the world of fact, which pre-exist to the establishment of

[1] One might find a nearer approach to a true hypothetical in an historical context: *e.g.*, if this is an eleventh-century building it cannot
have been an offshoot of the adjacent twelfth-century monastic house:
but in making such a judgment the mind is groping after an historical
proposition and has not yet grasped it. When grasped, the situation
which is here hypothetically presented becomes "this *is* an eleventh-
century building, and therefore," etc.

that relation. How this can be, history does not ask. It asks questions only about its own object, not about the way in which it comes to know that object. In history thought does not return upon itself; just as the artist is too much absorbed in imagining to reflect upon his imagining (except perhaps in his spare time) so the historian is too much absorbed in his attempt to apprehend facts to reflect upon that attempt. No doubt the historian's studies bring him into the closest contact with a spiritual life akin to his own; he seeks to study the activities of the human spirit not by setting up imaginary instances of them, like the artist, nor yet by substituting for them a mechanical play of abstract types, like the psychologist, but by apprehending them in their full actuality, as they really exist in the world of fact. But these actual happenings are always the object of his thought, and never his thought itself. However closely he sympathises with the men whose acts he traces, however much akin to himself he feels them, they are no more than akin; the relation between him and the object of his thought is a relation at most of ὁμοιουσία, never ὁμοουσία. He is an historian, and those whom he studies are not historians: his interest in them, in the past, is not balanced by any interest that they may be thought to have reciprocally in him or similarly in their own past. Consequently he is always the spectator of a life in which he does not participate: he sees the world of fact as it were across a gulf which, as an historian, he cannot bridge. He may and ought to reflect that he, too, is a part of the world of fact, and that his own historical thought is a product of the historical process which he is studying; but this does not reduce history to the historian's self-knowledge, because within the system of fact, though each fact implies the others, each fact yet remains itself and there is a difference between studying one fact and studying another. To specialise in Alexander the Great does not by itself make the historian an authority on Napoleon; and in the same way, though he is part of the same world as Alexander and Napoleon, his knowledge of them is not *eo ipso* knowledge of himself. Even when he turns autobiographer he does not really know himself, for his actual historical thought, the thought that is active in the composition of the autobiography, eludes him. The historian is thus always thinking of an object other than his own historical thinking: hence history itself is always a different thing from the history of history, and the history of the history of history is a different thing again, and so *ad infinitum*. In all this, the difference between history and philosophy is clear: the philosopher's object is at once himself and his world, and hence philosophy and the philosophy of philosophy are identical. To philosophise is to face the question how we know; and this question is at the same time the question how we know that we know.

These various forms of thought (art, science, history, philosophy) are not species of a genus. All history is art, because to tell a story is art, whereas to tell a true story is history: thus history is art, but a specification of art, art qualified by a condition (truth) which deprives it of a part of its character but not of all. In one sense, the historian must not be imaginative: in another sense, imagination is his most necessary possession. This is not a mere ambiguity in the word imagination. The historian's imagination is precisely the same thing as the novelist's imagination; but whereas the artist imagines for the sake of imagining, the historian's imagination is a disciplined imagination, subordinated to the pursuit of truth. Again, the special activity of the scientist is to generalise; but the historian, as we have seen, generalises too, only he generalises not for the sake of generalising, like the scientist, but for the sake of helping himself to determine historical fact. Thus art and science are contained in history, not excluded from it: yet contained in a form transmuted by their subordination to the historical end. History, on the other hand, is not contained in this manner in art or science; the historical material of a novelist ceases to be history and becomes pure art by being imaginatively handled, and the historical material of a scientist—experiment and observation—ceases to be history by being torn from its context in the world of fact and regarded as so many mere instances of laws. No doubt the artist and scientist must in some sense be historians, just as the historian must in some sense be an artist and a scientist; but not in the same sense. The historian is suppressed in the artist and the scientist; the artist and scientist are preserved but subordinated in the historian. Similarly, the philosopher must in a sense be an historian and the historian in a sense a philosopher; but the philosopher is suppressed in the historian, and the historian is preserved but subordinated in the philosopher; history is included in philosophy while philosophy is excluded from history. This appears in a striking manner in the relation between philosophy and the history of philosophy. No one can be competent in philosophy without having studied closely and well some part of the history of philosophy, but in his actual philosophical thinking the question what view So-and-so held is subordinated to the question what view is true. But the sound historian of philosophy, though he must be reasonably competent in philosophy, is in point of fact often a third-rate philosopher, because he is compelled to desist from raising the question what philosophical view is true in order to concentrate his attention on the question what views have been held by certain persons.

History in its fundamental and elementary form is perception. Perception is the simplest case of historical thinking: it is the most elementary determination of fact. But all history, however advanced and elaborated, is an elaboration of perception, a development of elements already contained in perception: and the world as known to the historian is simply an enrichment of the world as given in perception. History is perception raised to its highest power, just as art is imagination raised to its highest power. Perception appears to the perceiver as immediate; this is what is meant by speaking of the object of perception as "given." But it is not in reality immediate, and its object is not in the strict sense given. Reflexion shows in all perception two elements, sensation and thought: thought "interpreting" or reflecting upon the "data of sensation." Sensation here is a mere abstraction, the limiting case in which we are supposed to receive unreflectively a pure datum. In actual experience we never get such a pure datum: whatever we call a datum is in point of fact already interpreted by thought. The object of perception is a "given" which is itself an interpretation of a further "given" and so *ad infinitum*. The only difference between what we ordinarily call perception and what we ordinarily call historical thinking is that the interpretative work which in the former is implicit and only revealed by reflective analysis is in the latter explicit and impossible to overlook. History is sometimes said to be an inferential superstructure built upon perceptual data; but this conveys the impression that history and perception are two distinct activities, the one mediated by thought, the other immediate. This is an error, due to the fact that the thought which is explicit in history is only implicit in perception: for in all perception we are making a judgment, trying to answer the question what it is that we perceive, and all history is simply a more intense and sustained attempt to answer the same question. The past events which the historian brings to light are only revealed by his thought in its attempt to understand the world present to his senses: a past event which has left no trace on his perceptible world is to him unknowable. Seeing a light patch on the horizon and asking what it is, one may reply, it is a snow mountain: seeing a mottled object on the table and asking what it is, one may reply, it is a thirteenth-century charter. The processes involved are more elaborate in the latter case than in the former, but in the principle they are not different.

All perception depends on past experience. We only identify that which we perceive as this or that by comparing our present experience with past experience; and we perceive more and more accurately according as we become more and more able to compare the present experience with relevant experiences in the past. We are not always explicitly conscious of doing this, but im- plictly we do it whenever we perceive; and when we are faced with a difficult problem in perception we tend to do it explicitly. In these cases it becomes clear that perception rests on memory. We give ourselves the best chance of perceiving aright in diffi- cult cases by remembering relevant perceptions in the past: and the effort to remember, or recollection, is therefore an effort to supply ourselves with materials for present perception. Hence we may prepare for solving future perceptual problems by stor- ing our memory with relevant instances, and assisting it by taking notes of what we wish to recollect. Such collections of instances, in the form of oral tradition or written notes, become a body of corporate memories by which one man's experience may assist not only himself but others: and this is the germ of historical sources and documents. Memoirs, the accounts of things per- ceived by the writer himself, are the simplest and most ele- mentary form of written history. In reading memoirs we are not so much using our own experience of life in order to understand what we find written, as using what we find written in order to enrich and deepen our own experience of life. But once we make this use of a single man's memoirs, we are in principle making use of anybody's and everybody's memoirs; we are committed to the study of records of other people's experiences, and this in- volves the question of supplementing one person's experience by another's. But the experience in question is perceptual experi- ence, and therefore subject to the distinction between truth and falsehood: hence we have not only to read, but to criticise. The recognition of this truth is what differentiates history in the higher sense of the word from the mere absorption and repeti- tion of stories: the historian in the higher sense is the man who is not content to accept what he is told but endeavours to criticise his sources in order to discover, so far as he can, whether they tell the truth. This critical work is sufficiently difficult to require

a somewhat elaborate training, which involves the incidental
construction of a host of sciences subsidiary to history; these are
commonly called, in the widest sense of the phrase, historical
methods. As the word method suggests, these sciences consist of
empirical generalisations or rules of procedure, instructing the
student how to proceed in typical cases. Of the construction of
such sciences there is in the nature of the case no end; for each
has value only in relation to a certain arbitrarily-limited field of
inquiry. Their business is to solve the problem "how can the
historian check his sources?" to which the general answer is, "the
historian who knows his business can always invent methods of
checking any source." This would be impossible if the historian's
work consisted simply of arguing from given data; but we have
already seen that there is no such thing as a given datum. The
historian's data consist of what he is able to perceive; and if he
can perceive little, no one but himself is to blame. The better
historian he is, the more his sources mean to him: and an infinitely good historian would have at his disposal an infinite
quantity of infinitely reliable evidence on any given point. This
is no empty ideal; it is one progressively realised. No competent
historian who reflects on the progress of his own thought can
overlook the way in which that progress has created[2] masses of
evidence bearing on questions concerning which there was once
no evidence whatever. It is, however, a truth easily overlooked if
we regard history from the academic point of view, the tendency
of which is to treat the "sources" for a given period as consisting
of a finite number of facts capable of being set before the student
in a source-book and not susceptible of any interpretation which
has not been already suggested. It follows that there are in history
no insoluble problems. A problem only exists for the historian
in so far as something in his experience has raised it; and in
the case of any *bona fide* problem—as distinguished from the

[2] *Created*, not *discovered*, because evidence is not evidence until it
makes something evident.

pseudo-problems which may be raised verbally out of idleness
but are not actually raised by historical thinking in the course of
its development—the way in which it arises must of necessity, to
an intelligent mind, convey some hint of the direction in which
evidence for its solution is to be sought. If history had been the
mere determination of any and every past event, it would be full
of insoluble problems: what, for instance, was the name of the
first Roman citizen who died a natural death in the year 1 A.D.?
His name was just as much a fact as the name of the Emperor
then reigning: but before his name can become a problem to
historical thought, the problem must arise within historical
thought; it must, that is to say, arise somehow out of the attempt to perceive more adequately the world that exists here
and now for our perception. The infinite whole of fact which
it is the historian's business to determine is—and this is crucial for a sound philosophy of history—a world whose centre
is the historian's "immediate" perception, and whose radius is
measured by the depth to which he can see into the significance
of that perception. Hence there is in the last analysis no distinction between his sources and his conclusions; his conclusions, as
soon as he has reached them, become his sources, and all his
sources are conclusions which he has reached. The distinction
between sources and conclusions is a provisional distinction arising out of the distinction between problems solved and problems
as yet unsolved; that historical judgment is a conclusion, out of
which as yet no new problem has arisen.

If the radius of every historian's world were infinite, the
world of each historian would coincide with that of every other.
But this does not happen. The world of every historian is limited
by the limits of his knowledge: and because no two historians
start from the same "data of immediate perception," the circum-
ferences of their worlds must always fail to coincide. Any two
historians will find that they share a large number of interests, of
problems, of beliefs, but that each has a number of problems,

urgent for himself, which for the other are wholly non-existent.
This fact, which is called specialisation, is familiar enough, but
it is not always recognised to be a necessary implication of the
historical consciousness; indeed, people who believe that the
business of history is merely to discover the past in its entirety
are unable to understand it and apt to emphasise their failure by
deploring it.

Each historian sees history from his own centre, at an angle of
his own: and therefore he sees some problems which no other
sees, and sees every problem from a point of view, and therefore
under an aspect, peculiar to himself. No one historian, therefore, can see more than one aspect of the truth; and even an
infinity of historians must always leave an infinity of aspects un-
seen. Historical study is therefore inexhaustible; even the study
of a quite small historical field must necessarily take new shape
in the hands of every new student. This, we may observe, is not
subjective idealism, unless it is subjective idealism to maintain
that a hundred people looking at the same tree all see different
aspects of it, each seeing something hidden from the rest. The
more their perception is an intelligent perception, impregnated
with thought, the more nearly true it will be to say that each sees
what the others see, and that all see not merely an apparent tree
but the real tree; but they can never detach themselves from the
distinct starting-points at which they took up the process of perceiving. So the various "perspectives" of historians are arranged
in a "space of perspectives"; each historian is a monad which
mirrors the universe from a point of view that is irrevocably not
any other's point of view.

And the historian's own point of view is not constant. The
world he perceives is a world perpetually changing not simply
by the increase of its radius but by the displacement of its centre.
His problems change not only as one is solved and in its solution
generates another, but also because problems cease to interest him
before he has solved them finally. He is always "giving up"

riddles as well as answering them; indeed, the way in which he deals with every actual riddle is a compromise between answering it and giving it up. Hence no single historical problem is ever finally solved. All history at its actual best is the provisional and tentative answer to a question which remains at bottom unanswered. The actual and the ideal do converge; the historian does get nearer to a real knowledge of the infinite world of fact; but they converge asymptotically. The nearer the actual comes to the ideal, the greater becomes the force, generated by this very approach, to prevent a still closer convergence. The more the historian knows, the more acutely he becomes aware that he will never really know anything, and that all his so-called knowledge is to an unverifiable extent erroneous. Fact, in its reality, is unknowable.

Thus, in so far as he reflects upon his own historical thinking, the historian learns the merely monadic nature of his own thought. But a monad has no windows, and the historian as such cannot do the work of co-ordinating the infinity of possible perspectives. He can only travel from one perspective to another. He can never get outside his own point of view and see it as a monad among monads. He is a monad, not a monadologist; that is to say, he is a necessary victim of the "egocentric predicament" which holds good of all perception. This is because of what we called the objectivity of history. The historian thinks about his object, not about his own awareness of his object; he thinks not about his point of view but from his point of view. But in reflecting, that is philosophising, about his own thought he recognises that he is a monad, and to realise that one is in the "egocentric predicament" is to transcend it. When thought returns upon itself and faces the question of its own relation to its object, by criticising the point of view from which it has regarded that object it transcends this point of view.

Hence to philosophise about historical thinking is to transcend the monadism of historical thought, to desert monadism for monadology, to see not merely a perspective but the space of perspectives. History is finite thinking, because in its concentration upon its object it suppresses the question of its relation to that object; philosophy is infinite thinking because in philosophy the question what its object is coincides with the question of the relation between its object and itself. Philosophy cancels the finitude of history simply by recognising it.

The world of fact, which for history is an external presupposition of thought, becomes for philosophy a world of perspectives each having at its centre an historical consciousness; a world of worlds of thought each relative to its thinker. This world of worlds is a world which has no centre; its centre is everywhere and its circumference is nowhere; and in it there is no such thing as a presupposition of thought except in the sense that thought itself is its own presupposition.

Oswald Spengler and the Theory of Historical Cycles*

SINCE PLATO ANNOUNCED that the course of history returned upon itself in 72,000 years, since Polybius discerned a "circular movement" by which the history of states came back, over and over again, to the same point, the theory of historical cycles has been a commonplace of European thought. Familiar to the thinkers of the Renaissance, it was modified by Vico in the early eighteenth century and again by Hegel in the early nineteenth; and a complete history of the idea would show many curious transformations and cover a long period of time. Here no attempt will be made to summarise this story; the subject of the present paper is the latest and, to ourselves, most striking exposition of the general theory, contained in Dr. Oswald Spengler's *Decline of the West.*[1]

Spengler's view of history presents it as a succession of cultures, each having a peculiar physiognomy of its own which it maintains and works out down to the smallest details, and each following a definite course of development through a sequence of phases that is identical for all. Every culture has its spring, its

---

* Reprinted from *Antiquity* (1927), with the permission of the editor.
[1] *Untergang des Abendlandes* (1918). I quote from the admirable English translation (Allen and Unwin, 1926).

dawning phase, economically based on rural life and spiritually recognisable by a rich mythological imagination expressing in epic and legend the whole world view which, later, is to be developed in philosophical and scientific form. Then follows its summer, at once a revolt against the mythology and scholasticism of the spring and their continuation; a period in which a young and vigorous urban intelligence pushes religion into the background and brings to the fore a strictly scientific form of consciousness. The autumn of the culture pushes this consciousness to its limit, while at the same time it sees the decay of religion and the impoverishment of inward life; rationalism, enlightenment, are its obvious marks. Last comes winter, the decay of culture and the reign of civilisation, the materialistic life of the great cities, the cult of science only so far as science is useful, the withering of artistic and intellectual creativeness, the rise of academic and professional philosophy, the death of religion, and the drying-up of all the springs of spiritual life. The four-fold distinction of phases is not a necessity; at times it is convenient to distinguish more or fewer than four; but however many are distinguished in one culture the same number is necessarily distinguishable in all others. Thus, the revolt against Gothic which we call the Renaissance is a morphologically necessary phase of our culture; it is called the exhaustion of the early or primitive phase of a culture and the rise of the conscious or urban phase in which the individual working for himself takes the place of the anonymous corporate effort of the springtime. And therefore the same thing must happen in all cultures; in Egypt it is the revolt against the "pyramid style," in Greece the close of the archaic period, and so forth. Again, Napoleon in the western culture marks the exact point of transition from autumn to winter, from culture proper to civilisation; the break-up of the state proper and the beginning of imperialism, the victory of the great city over the country, the triumph of money over politics. Hence Napoleon is

OSWALD SPENGLER AND HISTORICAL CYCLES

exactly parallel (or, as Spengler calls it, "contemporary") with Alexander, who marks the transition from the Hellenic world to the Hellenistic; in no sense parallel with Caesar, who marks a phase *within* the "winter" period, and is "contemporary" with a phase in western history that still lies in the future. The point which we have now reached is the plutocracy disguised by demagogism, and called "democracy," which is represented by the second century B.C. in Rome.

Thus the cycle repeats itself in the smallest details, every phase reappearing in every cycle; yet what reappears is never the same phase—nothing can happen twice—but only something *homologous* with it, something which in the new cycle corresponds structurally with something in the old. Here comparative anatomy is the clue. A whale and an elephant lead radically different lives; everything about each is adapted to its own life; a whale is altogether whale and an elephant is elephantine through and through; but every organ and every bone in the one is homologous with an organ or a bone in the other. The task of morphology is to grasp at once the homology or correspondence of parts, and their differentiation by the fundamental difference between the two species. Merely to say "this bone in the elephant reminds me of that in the whale," is unscientific; and it is equally unscientific to say "a whale and an elephant are so different that nothing is gained by comparing them." Similarly it is unscientific merely to mention likenesses in history, a likeness between Alexander and Caesar, or between Buddha and Christ; and equally unscientific to say that the differences between cultures are so profound as to make likenesses impossible. The only scientific thing to do is to recognise at once the likeness and the difference, combining them into the notion of a homology or structural identity. We then see that Alexander and Caesar cannot be homologous, for they fall in the same culture; one closes its autumn, the other helps, though not crucially, to consolidate its winter; and that Buddha and Christ are still less to be compared, because the latter marks the creative spring of the Arabian culture, the former, the congealing winter of the Indian.

This conception is set forth at enormous length in a formless and chaotic volume, heavy with erudition and illuminated by a brilliant play of analogical insight, and a still more brilliant power of discrimination. The unforgettable things in the book are the passages in which the author characterises such fundamental differences as those between classical things and their modern analogues: in which he illustrates the thesis that "Classical culture possessed no memory, no organ of history in the highest sense," or that the ancients thought of space as the non-existent—this he proves not simply by quoting philosophers but by analysing sculpture and architecture—whereas western man regards infinite space as his true home and proper environment; which again is proved not from Kant but from a study of Gothic and oil-painting. For the philosopher only makes explicit in his own peculiar way an idea which has necessarily been the common heritage of his entire culture; and nothing is more admirable than the way in which Spengler sees and expounds this important truth.

The strange thing is that he seems to think his ideas altogether new. Learned as he is, he is either very ignorant or very reticent concerning the history of his own science. He asserts over and over again that the morphology of historical cultures is a wholly new thing. He seems ready to admit, in a single cautious sentence, that with regard to political history the idea is old; but he denies that anyone has applied it to "*all* branches of a culture." That may be; all is a large word; but if he really knew of the cyclical doctrines of Plato, Polybius, Machiavelli, and above all Vico, which last both anticipates his own in all essentials and goes far beyond it in historical profundity; if he even knew of Professor Petrie's recent and fascinating exposition of the same doctrine, he cannot be acquitted of *suppressio veri*. He cannot claim to have omitted them for lack of space; his book consists largely of repetitions, and of its 250,000 words it would have been easy to devote 250 to naming his predecessors in the field. The fact that he has not done so, makes it incumbent on a critic like the present writer to confess that not only has the main thesis of Spengler's book been familiar to him all his life, but that the reading of it has not given him a single genuinely new idea; for all the applications of the thesis are mechanical exercises which, so far as the present writer is acquainted with the ground, he has long ago carried out for himself. This one may say without claiming to possess a quarter of Spengler's erudition.

This erudition, gigantic as it is, shows one gap. Spengler is at his worst in discussing philosophy. He shows what must be called a complete misunderstanding of Plato when he mistakes a deliberately "mythical" literary form for a "mystical" type of thought (what philosopher was ever less "mystical" than Plato?); he consistently attributes to the Stoics the fundamental conception of the Epicureans, and incidentally misunderstands its meaning; and he commits the appalling blunder of asserting that for Descartes the soul is in space—a statement which falsifies the whole modern conception of the relation between space and thought and goes far to explain his long rambling polemics against what he takes to be the philosophy of Kant.

This is not a matter of mere ignorance concerning one department of human history. He is not all ill-informed on the history of philosophy, he is ill at ease in philosophy itself; and this means that whenever he tries to handle a fundamental problem he does so clumsily and without firmness or penetration. Brilliant on the surface, glittering in its details with a specious cleverness and apparent profundity, his "philosophy of history" is at bottom lacking in orientation, unsound on fundamentals, ill thought-out, and in consequence committed to a method which falsifies even its detail when a crucial case arises. These are serious charges; they are only made because Spengler's is a serious book which

deserves to be taken seriously; and the first step towards proving
them must be to quote falsified details. They are numerous; here
are a few.

"The Greek and Roman alike sacrificed to the gods of the place
in which he happened to stay or reside; all other deities were
outside his range of vision" (p. 83). This *must* be true, because
it follows from the fundamentally spaceless and timeless character of the classical mind, its insistence on the here-and-now as
the only reality. But it is *not* true. Even Odysseus prays to his
own Athene as he struggles for life in the stormy sea; and the
Roman carries to the ends of the empire the Juppiter Optimus
Maximus of the Capitol. The first half of Spengler's sentence is
true; the second is false. This means that he has represented as
the whole of the classical mind what was in reality only a part.
The tendency to worship the gods of the land was very real; but
it was only one tendency, and it was constantly balanced and
checked by a counter-tendency to carry with one the cult of one's
own place. *Caelum non animum mutant, qui trans mare currunt.*

Similarly, he asserts more than once that the classical mind was
essentially polytheistic, and opposes to it "Magian monotheism"
(p. 404), that is, alleges that monotheism is characteristic of the
Arabian culture that filled the first millennium of our era. But
this is, once more, inaccurate. All the Greek philosophers, until
the decadence, were monotheists; and Spengler knows that philosophy is only a reasoned statement of ideas common to the culture. The monotheism of the philosophers can only indicate a
profound strain of monotheism in the whole Graeco-Roman
world. And indeed Spengler himself would recognise that strain
(for its existence is notorious enough) did not his faulty logic
compel him to ignore it in the interests of his morphology.

Again, to take another example from ancient religion, he asserts that classical gods are all gods of the "near" and the "concrete," *numina* resident in things that are here-and-now, this
hearth, this door, this field, this river; this act, whether the act

of sowing or the act of love-making; always the sensuously present and near, never the distant or the future. "It is a deeply significant fact that in Hellas of all countries star-gods, the numina
of the Far, are wanting" (p. 402). We say nothing of the Sol
Invictus, the Mithras, of Imperial Rome; for with Imperial Rome
the author can play heads I win, tails you lose; in one aspect it
is the decadence of the "Classic," in another the rise of the
"Magian," and Mithras is obviously Magian. But has he forgotten Zeus-Juppiter the sky-god? Has he forgotten the stellar deities of Plato and the philosophical sky-worship of Xenophanes?
Has he forgotten that the adjective selected by himself as the
most perfectly descriptive of the classical mind is "Apollinian"?

These are not superficial flaws. They are not minor errors or
inconsistencies such as must exist in any great work. They are
sacrifices of truth to method; they are symptoms of a logical fallacy which underlies the whole book and has actually been erected
into a principle. The fallacy lies in the attempt to characterise a
culture by means of a single idea or tendency or feature, to deduce everything from this one central idea without recognising
that a single idea, asserted in this way, calls up its own opposite
in order to have something to assert itself against, and henceforth
proceeds, not by merely repeating itself, but by playing a game
of statement and counter-statement with this opposite. Everything in the classical mind is by Spengler deduced from the here-
and-now of the immediate, sense-given, bodily present. But to
assert the present is to deny the absent; therefore the absent must
be present to the classical mind as *that which it is denying,* and
it is impossible to concentrate one's mind on denying anything
unless one vividly feels the need of denying it; feels that it is
there to be denied, that someone, or some obscure force within
oneself, is asserting it. Further, when one has denied it, and denied it effectively and overwhelmingly, it reasserts itself in a new
form; and one has to begin over again, in order to meet this new
peril. So the attempt to frame a whole life—political, artistic, re-

ligious, scientific, and so forth—by working out the implications of a single fundamental idea is foredoomed to failure; the idea can only live in conflict with its own opposite, and unless that opposite is present as an effective force there is no conflict and no life.

This conception of the mind's life as a conflict between opposing ideas or tendencies is, nowadays, one would have thought, a commonplace. Indeed, Spengler himself says it is. It is the more curious that he should not himself possess the conception; or rather, that he should base his entire system of historical cycles on denying it. For this is what, in effect, he does. It is true that classical art or thought tends to be easily intelligible, while modern or western tends to be obscure to the many and intelligible only to the few; therefore, says Spengler, this is the whole truth; "everything that is classical is comprehensible in *one* glance"; instead of obscure philosophers, for instance, the classical world has philosophers who can be understood by the man in the street: and in this context he actually mentions Heraclitus, without adding that he was nicknamed "the Obscure" (p. 327). Magian monotheism is dualistic, therefore Jewish religion, being Magian, opposes to Jahweh (whom? you would never guess)—Beelzebub (p. 312)! The classical culture only cared for the present, therefore the Hellenes, unlike the Vikings, did not bury their dead in great barrows (p. 333); and what of the tombs on the Via Appia? Magian ethics, unlike Western, were mildly "recommended," not imposed as a command (p. 344); "the glad tidings of Jesus, like those of Zoroaster, of Mani, of Mahomet, of the Neo-Platonists and of all the cognate Magian religions were mystic benefits *displayed* but in no wise imposed." And did Islam never appeal for its extension to the help of the sword? Classical art creates an object to be beheld, a thing standing complete here-and-now, not entering, therefore, into any relation with the beholder or soliciting his attention (p. 329); what of the *parabasis* of Aristophanic drama? These are merely examples of the way in which, to bring them into the scheme, facts are constantly impoverished, robbed of one element merely because it is recessive, in order that the other, dominant as it is, may be erected into a false absolute. No one, probably, will deny that the elements which Spengler identifies as characteristic of this or that culture really are characteristic of it; where he fails is in thinking out what he means by "characteristic." He thinks that the characteristic is a fundamental something whose logical consequences flow smoothly and unopposedly into all its manifestations; whereas it is really the dominant partner in a pair of opposites, asserting itself only so far as it can keep its opposite in check and therefore always coloured by the hidden presence and underground activity of this opposite. To see the dominant characteristic and miss the recessive is to see history with the eye of the superficial student.

The same fault comes out in a different way in his view of the relation of cultures to one another. Vico, whose work he so curiously ignores, pointed out that the feudal barbarism of the Middle Ages differed from the Homeric feudal barbarism because it contained in itself Christianity, which summarises and transcends ancient thought (Croce, *Vico*, E.T. p. 132). And even Spengler, when it comes to mathematics, notices that Euclidean geometry is still retained today as elementary or school geometry, so that modern mathematics contains and transcends Greek mathematics. But though he sees this fact, he does not understand it; for him, every culture is just radically different from every other, based on its own idea and not on the idea of any but itself. Each culture is wholly self-enclosed; within its limits, it proceeds on a type-pattern exactly like that of the rest, but this similarity of structure is its *only* relation to the rest. For him, therefore, it is a misfortune that our elementary geometry is still Euclidean; it gets us into bad mathematical habits and sets an unnecessary obstacle in the way of our understanding modern non-Euclidean geometry. Thus the whole idea of "classical education" is, we infer, a gigantic blunder. Similarly, it was a misfortune, he thinks, that the "Magian" culture grew up under the tutelage of decaying classical civilisation, whose petrified relics prevented the new culture from rising spontaneously, because unopposed, in the Roman Imperial age. But surely it is not very hard to see that non-Euclidean geometry is based upon Euclidean even while it transcends and opposes it; and that the "Magian" culture, far from being stifled by the Roman Empire, used it as a scaffolding for its own building, a trellis for its own climbing flowers. The reason why Spengler denies these obvious facts is because he cannot grasp the true dynamic relation between opposites; his philosophical error leads him into the purely historical blunder of thinking that one culture, instead of stimulating another by its very opposition, can only crush it or be crushed by it. He thinks of cultures atomistically, each as a self-contained or closed system, precisely as Epicurus thought of the "worlds" whose plurality he asserted; and just as Epicurus could do nothing better with the spaces between his worlds than to hand them over to the gods as a dwelling, surrendering all attempt to make sense of the relation between world and world, so Spengler plugs the gap between one culture and the next with a crude, cultureless human life which insulates each culture from its neighbours and makes it impossible to envisage an historical whole of which every culture is a part. He actually claims that the abandonment of the historical whole, and the atomistic view of cultures, is a grand merit of his system; and so it is, for it cuts out the real problem of history, the problem of *interrelating* the various cultures, which is the problem that requires profound and penetrating thought, and leaves only the problem of *comparing* them, a far easier task for those shallow minds that can accept it. And if, as Spengler says, this is the age of shallow and decadent thought, of unphilosophical philosophy and unscientific science, his philosophy of history is, as he says it is, precisely what our age needs.

The fact is that Spengler, with all his erudition and historical learning, lacks the true historical mind. Learning does not make the historian; there is a *sense* of history which is not acquired through erudition, and for this historical sense we look to Spengler in vain. History deals with the individual in all its individuality; the historian is concerned to discover the facts, the whole facts, and nothing but the facts. Now comparative anatomy is not history but science; and Spengler's morphology is simply the comparative anatomy of historical periods. The historical morphologist is concerned not to discover what happened, but, assuming that he knows what happened, to generalise about its structure as compared with the structure of other happenings. His business is not to *work at* history, but to *talk about* it, on the assumption that someone else has already done the work—the work, that is, of finding out what the facts are, the historian's work. In this sense, Spengler nowhere shows the slightest desire to do a piece of historical work, or the slightest sign of having done one. His history consists of ready-made facts which he has found in books; and what he wants to do is to arrange these in patterns. When the man with historical sense reads a statement in a history book, he at once asks, is that really so? What evidence is there? How can I check the statement? and he sets to work doing over again, for himself, the work of determining the fact. This is because the historical sense means the feeling for historical thought as living thought, a thought that goes on within one's own mind, not a dead thought that can be treated as a finished product, cut adrift from its roots in the mind that thinks it, and played with like a pebble. Now the extraordinary thing about Spengler is that, after giving us a penetrating and vivid description of the difference between history and nature, and setting up the demand that we shall envisage "the world as history"—an admirable demand admirably stated—he goes on to consider the world not as history but precisely as nature, to study it, that is to say, through scientific and not historical spectacles, and to substitute for a truly genetic narrative, which would be history, a self-confessed morphology, which is science. And he is forced into doing this by his own philosophical errors, his errors, that is to say, concerning the structure of his own thought. He prepares us for all this, it is true, by his open scorn of logic and his statement that Goethe and Nietzsche are his only two masters; for neither Goethe nor Nietzsche, with all their poetic gifts and fine intelligence, had any grasp on the distinction between nature and history. And Spengler himself praises Goethe for confusing the two, for treating Nature as history and a culture as an organism.

The touchstone of the historical sense is the future. Science determines the future, foretells an eclipse or the like, just because the object of science is Nature and "Nature has no history." The laws of Nature are timeless truths. For history, time is the great reality; and the future is the infinite well-spring of those events which, when they happen, become present, and whose traces left upon the present enable us to reconstruct them when they are past. We cannot know the future, just because the future has not happened and therefore cannot leave its traces in the present. The historian who tries to forecast the future is like a tracker anxiously peering at a muddy road in order to descry the footsteps of the next person who is going to pass that way. All this, the historian knows instinctively. Ask him to forecast a single instant of the future, and he will laugh in your face. If anyone offers to foretell events, he speaks not as an historian but as a scientist or a clairvoyant. And if he offers to foretell events by means of historical thinking, he is either hoaxing his audience or saying historical when he means scientific. Spengler again and again claims that his morphology enables him to foretell the future. He even says that therein lies its chief merit and novelty; in which context, as usual, he refrains from mentioning his predecessors, the crowd of sociological writers, led by Marx, who have made just that claim.

But his claim to foretell the future is absolutely baseless. Just as his morphology does not work at history but only talks about it, does not *determine* the past but, assuming it as already determined, attaches labels to it, so this same method does not determine the future, but only provides a set of labels—the same old set—for a future that is undetermined. For instance, Spengler tells us that between A.D. 2000 and 2200 someone will arise corresponding to Julius Caesar. Well, we ask, what will he do? Where will he live? What will he look like? Whom will he conquer? All Spengler can say is, he will correspond to Julius Caesar; he will do the kind of things that a person would do, who corresponded to Julius Caesar; he will live in a place corresponding to Julius Caesar's Rome; he will look like a person corresponding to Julius Caesar, and so forth. But, we must reply, this is not predetermining history. Suppose, instead, it were a question of the past: suppose we asked, who corresponded to Julius Caesar in the Egyptian culture? Suppose, now, we were told, "oh, the answer is easy: the person who corresponded to Julius Caesar." This would be *the wrong answer*: it would have determined nothing: it would be a mere confession of ignorance concerning the Egyptian past. The *right* answer (Spengler has given it) would be "Thutmosis III." This is a real answer because it names an actual concrete individual in actual concrete circumstances; and until we can do that, we have not determined any history at all. But if the past is not determined until we have said "Thutmosis III," the future is not determined until we can say "John Jones of Bulawayo," or whoever it will be. Spengler's claim to foretell the future is on a par with saying that the possession of a clock will enable its possessor to foretell the future because he can say that twelve will happen an hour after eleven. No doubt; but what will be going on at twelve?

There is another reason why the claim is wholly futile. On his own showing, the decay of classical culture in Rome synchronised with the rise of Magian culture in the very same culture-area. Thus cultures may overlap both in space and in time. In Hadrian's reign, then, a Spengler might have diagnosed a general petrification and decay of everything classical, and said that the Roman world was a dying world. And when someone pointed to the Pantheon, and said, "is that a symptom of decay?" the answer would be, "that is an example of imperial display by means of material and mass" (see table II at the end of the book), "and therefore it is meaningless, barren, vulgar civilisation-architecture." But a counter-Spengler would retort, "not at all; the Pantheon is *the first Mosque* (pp. 72, 211, 358—as usual, he says it three time over) "and therefore belongs to the exuberant springtime of a nascent culture." Now it follows from the atomistic view of cultures that a new culture may begin anywhere, at any moment, irrespective of any circumstances whatever; and there is no possible proof that one is not beginning now. But if so, what becomes of "predetermining the future"?

It is all the more hopeless because there is no possible way, according to Spengler, of discovering what will be the fundamental idea of any hitherto undeveloped or unexamined culture. This, of course, follows from the atomistic conception; but its results are very serious. If any two cultures happened to have the same fundamental idea, they would be indistinguishable; the person corresponding to Julius Caesar would be Julius Caesar himself, repeated identically, name and all, at another date. That this possibility follows logically from Spengler's conception shows how profoundly anti-historical that conception is; that he has not observed it to follow, shows how ill he has thought out his own position. But on the other hand, if the fundamental idea of one culture differs from that of another, how can the one understand the other? Spengler unhesitatingly answers, it cannot. We do not understand the classical world; what we see in it is our own image in an opaque mirror. Very well, but how does he know this to be merely our image? How does he know that we are not understanding the past as it really was? There is no answer, and can be no answer; for the fact is, unless we understand the ancients well enough to know that we do not understand them completely, we can never have reason to suspect that our errors about them are erroneous. Spengler, by denying the possibility of understanding other cultures than our own, has denied the possibility of history itself. Here again, bad philosophy—a crude half-baked, subjective idealism—brings its own punishment. If history is possible, if we can understand other cultures, we can do so only by re-thinking for ourselves their thoughts, cherishing within us the fundamental idea which framed their lives; and in that case their culture lives on within ours, as Euclidean geometry lives on within modern geometry and Herodotean history within the mind of the modern historian. But this is to destroy the idea of atomic cultures, and to assert not a mere plurality of cultures but a unity of that plurality, a unity which is the present culture, the heir of all its past. Against that conception Spengler struggles, because, having no historical sense, he does not *feel* it, and, being a bad philosopher, cannot understand it; yet that conception is presupposed on every page of his work. "The unities of place, time and action" I read, opening it at random, "are . . . an indication of what classical man felt about life" (p. 323). And how does Spengler know what classical man felt? Only by putting himself into the position of classical man and feeling it too. Unless he has done that, he is deliberately deceiving us; no man knows what another feels if he is incapable of feeling it himself.

Spengler's so-called philosophy of history is therefore, we may repeat, lacking in orientation, because it reduces history to a plurality of cultures between whose fundamental ideas there is no relation whatever; it is unsound on fundamentals, because its purpose—that of "predetermining the future"—is impossible in itself and in any case unrealisable by his methods; it is ill thought-out, because he shows no signs of having seen the fatal objections to it; and it is committed to the methodical falsification of facts because it distorts every fact falling—or alleged to fall—within a given culture, into an example of an abstract and one-sided idea which is fancied to represent the essence of that culture. In all four respects, it is an unworthy child of the historical studies of the last two hundred years. In each respect it violates elementary dictates of the historical consciousness; in each respect it is far surpassed by the cyclical doctrines of Hegel, a hundred, and Vico, two hundred years ago. Vico realized that culture (to retain Spengler's term) could not arise by a miracle out of a uniform, purely cultureless, life; that barbarism contained the seeds of culture in itself, and produced culture by their germination. Thus Vico does away with Spengler's crude and superficial dualism between cultured and cultureless life. Further, granted that culture arises out of what Vico calls a "barbarism of sensation" and decays into a "barbarism of reflexion" (the latter being Spengler's civilisation), after having achieved a homogeneous development, economic and legal, religious and artistic, scientific and linguistic, Vico sees that this rule is merely approximate and not *a priori* necessary; he sees that there are exceptions to it, or, at least, that it is subject to such diversities of application in practice that it cannot serve as a basis for prophecy. This is, at bottom, because, the fundamental ideas of the various cultures being different, the cultures themselves will develop in different rhythms. Obviously, here Vico is right. What could be more ridiculous than Spengler's assumption that every idea will take the same number of years to develop through its different phases and exhaust its possibilities, no matter what idea it is? For that matter, why should it have the same phases at all? "We find," someone might plead, "that it does"; but Spengler is not entitled so to plead; for he asserts that a given culture *must* have passed through this or that phase, unknown though the phase may be, because others have done so.

Every culture, then, is surrounded not by sheer non-culture, but by other cultures, more or less perfect, perhaps, than itself; higher or lower, perhaps in the scale of value; but yet cultures. That is the first modification to be made in Spengler's doctrine.

Secondly, while recognising that a given culture has a certain self-consistent character, a fundamental idea which is working itself out into a complete social life, we must assert that this idea or character is not static but dynamic; it is not a single unchanged thing, miraculously born at one time, then persisting unaltered, and finally wiped out of existence, but a process of spiritual development, an idea which grows out of other ideas, in an environment of other ideas, which asserts itself against these other ideas through a process of give-and-take in which it modifies them and is modified by them in turn. In this process, culminating points are reached in which a given idea seems to have achieved an absolute domination. Here the whole culture becomes brilliantly luminous with the light of this idea; luminous to itself, so far as its own human vehicles grasp the idea consciously, luminous to us, so far as we can re-create their idea within our minds and so see what their life meant to them. But the domination is never absolute. It is always a domination over something; there are always other ideas knocking at the gate, kept out by force, whose pressure against the ring-fence of cultural life is equal and opposite to the expansive force of the life within. So the highest summits of culture reveal a contradiction between what they assert and what they deny—Greek liberty resting on Greek slavery, capitalist wealth resting on capitalist poverty—and in the long run the mere attempt to work out the cultural idea consistently, to *live* it (rather than *think* it) to the full, destroys the culture. But the destruction of one culture is the birth of another; for there is no static entity called a culture, there is only a perpetual development, a development in which what has been won must be lost in order that something further may be won. And everything that is achieved in this process rests on the basis of all that has been achieved in its past phases.

Because this process is always the same, though always new, it is easy to find analogies and homologies between any part of it and any other. But when we cut it up into sections and say "here begins classical culture, and here it ends: here begins Magian culture, and here it ends," we are talking not about history but about the labels we choose to stick upon the corpse of history. Better historical thinking, deeper historical knowledge, would show us within the heart of classical culture, not a single unchanged idea, but a dynamic interplay of ideas, containing elements which, even quite early, prepare it for its conversion into Magian. It is bad history and bad philosophy alike to argue that because the Pantheon is Magian it is not classical. Follow that up, and you will find that nothing is classical. It is truer to say that the classical is not a style but an age, a process, a development, which led to the Magian by its own inner logic. Thus the Pantheon is *both* Magian *and* classical; it is classical in the act of *turning into* Magian. And this conception of "turning into," the conception of becoming, is (as Spengler himself industriously asserts, and industriously forgets) the fundamental idea of all history.

What, then, remains of the conception of historical cycles? Much; for though a "period" of history is an arbitrary fabrication, a mere part torn from its context, given a fictitious unity, and set in a fictitious isolation, yet, by being so treated, it acquires a beginning, and a middle, and an end. And we fabricate periods of history by fastening upon some, to us, peculiarly luminous point and trying to study it as it actually came into being. We find our eye caught, as it were by some striking phenomenon—Greek life in the fifth century, or the like; and this becomes the nucleus of a group of historical inquiries, asking how it arose and how it passed away; what turned into it, and what it turned into. Thus we form the idea of a period, which we call the Hellenic period; and this period will resemble the Byzantine period or the Baroque period *in being a period,* that is, in having a luminous centre preceded and followed by processes whose only interest to us at the moment is that they lead to and from it. From another point of view, the movement leading away from fifth-century

Greece, the "decline of Hellas," will figure as the movement leading up to the Hellenistic world. Was it, then, "really" a decline or an advance? Neither, because both; it was a becoming, a change, a development; and the historian's highest task is to discover *what* developed, through *what* phases, into *what*. If anyone is not interested in that question, he is not interested in history.

Thus the historical cycle is a permanent feature of all historical thought; but wherever it occurs, it is incidental to a point of view. The cycle is the historian's field of vision at a given moment. That is why it has been so often observed that history moves in cycles; that is why, when people have tried, as many have tried, to formulate a system of cycles, that shall be "objectively valid," valid apart from any momentary point of view, they have failed with a failure whose completeness and strikingness has always been proportional to the rigour with which they have pursued the project. In a short essay, slightly written, anyone can expound a plausible system of historical cycles. Perhaps the very length of Spengler's book, and the very learning that he has lavished upon it, are well spent in revealing, as no shorter or less learned work could have done, the impossibility of the task he has attempted.

The Theory of Historical Cycles*

WHEN HUCKLEBERRY FINN's religious education was taken in hand by the Widow and Miss Watson, his impressionable mind was at first strongly affected—in his own words, he was all in a sweat—on hearing the story of Moses. Later, his interest in Moses cooled off, because Miss Watson let out that Moses had been dead a considerable time, and Huckleberry Finn, as he explains, took no stock in dead men.

It was a very naïve reaction to history; but naïve reactions often reveal truths which are blurred by a more sophisticated attitude, and must somehow be recaptured before we can see things as they are. Huckleberry Finn may here stand as the babe or suckling out of whose mouth the historian is to learn wisdom.

Moses is dead, and there is no need to get in a sweat about him. It is nobody's business to give him advice, or to advance or frustrate his schemes; nobody is called upon to work for him or against him, to excite himself about choosing to be pro-Moses or anti-Moses, to allow his feelings to be inflamed with partisanship or opposition, or even to commend or regret, applaud or condemn, label as good or bad. There is no sense in using terms like good and bad except of persons or things, that come into practical relations with one's own will. When Margaret Fuller an-

* Reprinted from *Antiquity* (1927), with the permission of the editor.

nounced that she "accepted the universe," Carlyle remarked, "Gad, she'd better"; meaning that there was no other sensible course to pursue; you couldn't reasonably call the universe good or bad, because you couldn't be "for" it or "against" it; the universe is not in need of our partisanship, nor in danger from our hostility; all it asks of us is that we should see it as it is, face it, accept it. Now that is all Moses asks of us. He is dead; the battles which he fought have long ago been won and lost, the causes that interested him have long ago been heard and judged. His work is done; friends cannot help him, enemies cannot hurt him; advocacy and malice are alike, for him, powerless. The only thing left for us to do is, if we can, to understand him: to "accept" him for what he was, to see how he lived and what he did when he was alive.

Does this mean that the historian is to give up using the words good and bad, to forget his moral principles and lose his sense of values, to renounce, in a word, the whole habit of getting in a sweat? In a sense, yes; in another sense, no. He certainly ought to give up labelling his *dramatis personae* as good and bad. Indeed, today no decent historian would hesitate about this; he gave it up long ago, and it only lingers in the slum-districts of historical thought—the dark places where history of a sort is bullied into the service of political and religious propaganda. But this does not mean forgetting his moral principles. On the contrary, it means remembering them with a quite new vigilance, but applying them not to the facile praise and blame of others—who are not in a position to reply—but to the harder task of controlling his own conduct. For, *qua* historian, he has a duty to perform; his duty is to discover the truth and tell it without fear or favour; and as a matter of fact the errors into which historians fall are never due to mere honest ignorance but always to some failure in their own sense of historical duty, some unfounded assumption or misplaced trust, or the cruder sin of anxiety to make a case or haste to finish writing a book. The historian who gets nearest to the truth is the historian who spends most pains in examining his conscience.

It may be suggested that we have here a principle capable of wider extension. The modern historian does not call Henry II a bad man because he quarrelled with Becket; and he would not admit that this forebearance betrays a weakness in his own moral standards; on the contrary, he would say it was a sign of moral soundness, of a highly moral determination to do Henry justice. Now why should we not extend this principle, say, to the history of art? Suppose someone to argue that a given period of art-history is a bad period, because its artists no longer show the same exquisite sensitiveness as those of an earlier age; may we not reply, "it is your business, not to deplore the lack of aesthetic sensitiveness in others, but to display it in your own person, by discovering the beauties of this art to which you have shown yourself blind"?

Two instances will make the point clear. In the eighteenth century, people of taste, who were not afraid to speak their mind, used the strongest possible language in describing the ugliness, the clumsiness, the tastelessness, of mediaeval architecture. Smollett, who was typical of his age, speaks of York Minster in terms expressive of sheer disgust.[1] He was perfectly sincere; and his very emphasis shows that it was a question not of an inartistic person's lack of interest in art, but of a person interested in architecture who feels that Gothic architecture is a blot upon the face of the earth. Two hundred years later, Professor Petrie[2] describes the sculpture and architecture of the thirteenth century as the cul-

---

[1] *Humphry Clinker* (Works, ed. 1806), p. 200. After describing the interior as a vast charnel-house, he goes on, "the external appearance of an old cathedral cannot be but displeasing to the eye of every man who has any idea of propriety or proportion," and especially objects to the "long slender spire," which "puts one in mind of a criminal impaled." It is safe to attribute Matthew Bramble's opinions to Smollett himself.

[2] *Revolutions of Civilisation* (1922), p. 60 etc.

mination, so far as concerns these arts, of all modern civilisation; as an achievement intrinsically almost equal to that of Graeco-Roman antiquity. Precisely where Smollett found the deepest degradation of modern art, Professor Petrie finds its loftiest triumph. Each writer fairly represents the general taste of his time, and each is a sincere and qualified spokesman of that taste. Which is right?

To say that Professor Petrie is right because he is our own contemporary would be to trust altogether too completely in the maxim *les absents ont toujours tort,* and involve the uncomfortable corollary that two hundred years hence, or less, Professor Petrie and ourselves will all be as wrong as Smollett is today. But how else are we to answer? Leibniz said that all philosophers were right in what they assert and wrong in what they deny; may we say that critics are always right when they assert the value of a period and always wrong when they deny it? At that rate, Smollett would be right to admire classical architecture, and right to admire the neo-classic of his own times, but wrong to deny all merit to mediaeval Gothic. The degradation of mediaeval art would thus be simply a blind spot in the eye of the beholder. If now we apply the same hypothesis to Professor Petrie, we find that, for him, the period of degradation comes between the classical and the mediaeval, and is represented by the incised figure of Bellicia on an early Christian slab in Rome.[3] Let us assume—it might be denied—that this slab is a fair and favourable example of an age which is also that of the Throne of Maximian and the consular diptychs; and then let us ask, is it possible that the utter badness of this art, like the utter badness of York Minster, depends merely on the critic's lack of sympathy? Is it conceivable that at some future date this Byzantine way of doing things (to give it that name for the sake of a name) may come to be recognised as a fundamentally right and good way, as the Gothic way

---

[3] *Ibid.,* p. 6 (fig. 2), p. 59.

of doing things came to be recognised by the work of the Romantic movement?

To ask the question is to answer it. Already, since Professor Petrie's book was written, the movement of fashion has set decisively towards Byzantine art, and plenty of aesthetes today will turn back to the picture of Bellicia as to one of the most impressive things in the book. Crude it is; unskilful; anatomically imperfect (so, for that matter, is the Ludovisi throne); yet the vigour of its drawing, the purposeful economy of its line, the intense and rapt expression of the full face and the upward gesture of the transfigured arms, give it an unearthly beauty that is not to be compared with the earthly beauty of the stele of Hegeso[4]—not as superior, nor as inferior, but as different. Here Spengler has improved upon Petrie; Byzantine art, which for Petrie seems to be a mere aberration, a trough between waves, a phase whose only qualities are negative qualities, varying kinds of badness, has become for Spengler a positive movement, authentically and eloquently expressing its own proper ideals.

Where the eighteenth century saw a trough, Professor Petrie sees a wave; where Professor Petrie sees a trough, Dr. Spengler sees yet another wave. Where is this process to end? Are there really an infinite number of waves, all overlapping each other, so that by the time one has sunk into its trough, its place has been taken by another, or quite a number of others successively?

"The dark ages," says Dean Inge, in his lecture on the Idea of Progress, "knew that they were dark." Did they? Did the Venerable Bede, and the carver of the Bewcastle cross, and John the Scot, called Eriugena, know that the spirit of their time condemned their search for knowledge and beauty to futility? There is a sense in which all human effort is futile, and every age dark; the greatest of Venetian painters died full of years and fame with on his lips the words: *e faticoso lo studio della pittura, e*

---

[4] *Ibid.*, p. 6 (fig. 1).

sempre si fa il mare maggiore; and Newton's comparison of himself to a child on the seashore might be taken as evidence that the classical age of modern physics was a dark age and knew it. But the darkest age is not so dark that men cannot see the next step before them; and the lightest age is no lighter.

Not only are there no dark ages, except in the sense in which every age is dark, and in the sense of ages which this or that historian dislikes and misunderstands, but there are, with the same two reservations, no decadences.

In history, *tout lasse, tout passe, tout casse*; everything decays, and all movement is a movement away from something, a loss of something won, a withering, a death. The growth of the steamship is the passing-away of that splendid thing, the sailing-ship; the rise of fire-arms is the decadence of archery; the rise of Christianity and the unearthly beauty of Bellicia is the death of Paganism and the earthly beauty of Hegeso. And it is perfectly correct to speak of the fifteenth century as the century of the decline of archery, of the sixteenth as the century of the decline of the manuscript book, of the seventeenth as that of the decline of polyphonic music, of the eighteenth as that of the decline of absolute monarchy, and of the nineteenth as that of the decline of the sailing-ship. It would seem, therefore, that European civilisation, expressing itself as it does through these various organs, has been dying by inches for an unconscionable time. Surely it owes a word of apology to the prophets gathered round its death-bed; if not in the style of King Charles, at least in that of Socrates, when to his friends' tearful question "where shall we bury you?" he replied, "where you will, if you can catch me." For this dying by inches is merely a synonym for life; when archery, or counterpoint, or the full-bottomed wig, shows symptoms of decay, that merely proves that the spirit of man is no longer in it; it is not here, it is risen; it has passed into another vehicle, and the mourners who bewail its death are all unaware that it is re-creating itself in a new form beneath their very eyes.

In that sense, every age is an age of decadence. The Romans of the great age of Caesar were right enough to lament the lost *mores maiorum*; they saw that in the splendid blossoming of the genius of their race something had perished; some moral quality, never to be replaced, whose loss could never be quite compensated, was gone. So the Athenians of the age of Phidias, had they cared for history as much as the Romans, might have known that their Maidens of two generations ago had a delicate and cryptic beauty that no Phidias could ever recapture. But, it is constantly maintained,—and this is the essence of every cyclical theory of history—some ages are ages of decadence pure and simple, ages of mere decadence, periods of decay *par excellence*. Michelangelo, doubtless, could not have carved the kings of Chartres, if he had tried; but he could do something as good, or better. Thorwaldsen could not have carved the tomb of Lorenzo; but also, he could not do anything as good. Therefore the decadence of sculpture sets in at some time after Michelangelo, and has made visible progress by the nineteenth century.

The answer to this is that though Michelangelo and Thorwaldsen are both called sculptors, they were not trying to do the same thing, and therefore the question which did it better does not arise. If we take a single art and study two different phases of its development, we always find them differentiated by a difference of the ideal aimed at. For instance, early Renaissance architecture aims at emphasising the structural lines of the building, the lines of thrust and stress; it makes its patterns out of these lines, so that the building seems to have its bones drawn on its surface. Baroque architecture, on the contrary, growing directly out of early Renaissance, deliberately conceals the bones of the building and revels in curved and twisted lines whose purpose is precisely to contrast with the lines of thrust which the architect and the intelligent spectator know to be there. Hence Baroque appeals to a different kind of mood, talks in a different language, strives after a different ideal, from early Renaissance.

Just as Baroque sculpture, in Bernini, delights in forgetting the hardness and brittleness of stone, and employs its virtuosity to make its marble soft like flesh, pliant like cord, or vibrant like foliage, so Baroque architecture deliberately conceals the engineering of its structures and makes them look as if they were moulded in a plastic material, and crowned with domes as imponderable as the rising moon. To say that one or other of these two ideals is inherently better than the other, to call this, in a derogatory sense, primitive, or that decadent, is to betray a merely personal predilection; or less indeed than personal, because certain not to survive honest personal scrutiny of the work supposed inferior. Once you come to see what the supposedly decadent school is driving at, you see that it has a legitimate and genuine problem of its own and is handling it in the only possible way. But before you have come to see that, you can only account for the facts by a theory of mere decadence: by supposing that the later people were trying to do the same thing as the earlier, but were unable to do it so well. This theory, it may be said without hesitation, is always false. It always shows failure to understand what the later people were driving at. To take a few examples: modern music may be called decadent relatively to Bach because no modern musician has the technical skill to write a Bach fugue. But no modern musician wants to; he wants to handle masses of orchestral colour, and by comparison with the orchestral colour-composition of Richard Strauss, that of Bach is crude to absurdity. Anglian sculpture may be said to decay after the Bewcastle cross; but the later sculptors were not trying, and failing, to reproduce the linear filigree-work of the early style; they were trying to move away from it to a style of broad poster-like effects,[5] to make a design that would "carry" across a churchyard; and from that point of view they improved vastly on the Bewcastle artist's achievement. Professor Petrie points to the decay in the drawing

[5] W. G. Collingwood, *Northumbrian Crosses*, p. 49.

of the hieroglyphic hawk in the sixth dynasty; but his examples suggest that the so-called "decadent" hawks are really graphic symbols far more convenient to the writer's hand than the naturalistic pattern which preceded them. The artist has stopped drawing and begun to write; or rather, he has ceased to allow his draughtsmanship to distract him from the work of writing.

From this point of view it is desirable to bestow a glance on the idea of progress.[6] In its crudest form—a form in which probably no one has ever maintained it—the idea of progress would imply that throughout history man has been working at the same problem, and has been solving it better and better. Now this is not wholly untrue. There is a sense in which, in any department of human life—politics, for instance, or poetry—there is only one single problem, constant throughout all ages. And if anyone asks why we do not revive the Greek city-state, we may fairly answer that it has been tried, and has served its turn, and we think we can do better than that nowadays. To say that, is to commit oneself to the doctrine of progress; not a mechanical or automatic progress, but a progress which is nothing but the corporate life of mankind remembering and learning by its own past; refraining from putting back the clock not because it cannot but because it will not, because it thinks the present, with all its draw-backs, better than anything it knows about the past.

Justice is not always done to this idea. There is more in it than is recognised by those—generally people with no very deep interest in history—who idealise this or that phase of the past and, because they only know its brighter side, think they would prefer it to the present; or by those utterly unhistorical minds that think they can eat their cake and have it too, that they could have Periclean Athens without the massacre of Melos and the Middle Ages without the Black Death. There is probably no one, deeply versed in any period of past history, who, if a fairy offered him

6 J. B. Bury, *The Idea of Progress*, gives an invaluable account of the growth and development of the idea.

the choice of going to live in that period or continuing to live in the present, would not prefer to live in the present.

But the choice cannot be offered, and the problem cannot arise. Moses is dead; and because the past is past, we cannot rationally either praise it at the expense of the present or decry it by comparison with the present. We ought not to call it either better than the present or worse; for we are not called upon to choose it or to reject it, to like it or to dislike it, to approve it or to condemn it, but simply to accept it. In one sense, the problem of politics is always the same; but there is an equally important sense in which it is always different. At one time the problem may be how to impose on a centrifugal society of feudal barons a single law and the centralised government of a single king; at another time, it may be how to create, in a too centralized country, bureaucracy-ridden and apathetic, some kind of local political initiative. These different problems call for different solutions, and it is meaningless to assert that the system of local government which meets the latter situation is either better or worse than the strong personal monarchy which meets the former. Each is, so far as it succeeds, absolutely the right solution for its own problem, and not relevant to any other. People with no eye for the intricacies of an actual political situation often deplore the "sentimental" ideals of modern democracy, and sigh for the strong hand of sixteenth-century monarchy; not realising that modern democracy can afford to assert freedom as it does precisely because the nations that accept its ideals have thoroughly learnt the lesson of obedience to law, and are now in more danger from despotism than from anarchy.

The business of the historian is to discover what problems confronted men in the past, and how they solved them. These problems were always in one sense identical with each other and with his own, and in another sense all different and unique; thus in one sense all history is one, and in another sense it is composed of an infinite number of distinct and at least provisionally sepa-

rable episodes. But however much an historian insists on the
unity of history, it is impossible for him to deny its plurality, the
gulf between any two phases in the past, due to mere lapse of
time, which creates changed circumstances and therefore demands different ways of reacting to them. And however much he
insists on its plurality, there is still some unity running through
it in virtue of which he calls it all history; it is held together sub-
jectively in the unity of his own historical thought, even if all
other bonds fail. But the objective bond of history is continuity.
This means that the solution of one problem is itself the rise of
the next. Man is not confronted by changing circumstances outside himself; or if he is, that belongs to the mere externals of his
life. The essential change is within himself; it is a change in his
own habits, his own wants, his own laws, his own beliefs and
feelings and valuations; and this change is brought about by the
attempt to meet a need itself arising essentially from within. It is
because man is not content to react automatically to the stimulus
of nature that he is man, and not a plant or a mere animal; his
humanity consists in his self-consciousness, his power to mould
his own nature, which comes simultaneously with his awareness
of that power. Man's action is the result of his dissatisfaction
with himself as he is; the result of the action is the creation of a
new self, and this new self gives rise to a new problem, and so
for ever. This succession of problems, each solved in the only
way in which it can be solved, because solved by the output of
all the powers at the agent's disposal, is the course of history.
The historian may not always be able to see it so, but that is the
way it always happens. Now such a course of events may be truly
called a progress, because it is a going forward; it has direction,
everything in it proceeds out of what has gone before and could
not have happened without the occurrence of its past. Every
detail of the past is somehow necessary to the being of the
present, and thus the present is truly built upon the past.

But though history is in this sense a progress and nothing but a progress, it cannot be so in any other sense. No one of the phases through which it moves is any better, or any worse, than any of the others. In each phase, men found themselves confronted by a unique situation, which gave rise to a unique problem, or the eternal problem in a unique form; in each phase, they did their best to solve this problem, for their whole life consisted simply in living, living under the peculiar circumstances which made life a problem of a peculiar kind. To live was to solve that problem, the condition of surviving until the problem changed; to die was to bequeath a different problem to their successors.

So far as we can see history as a whole, that is how we see it; as a continuous development in which every phase consists of the solution of human problems set by the preceding phase. But that is only an ideal for the historian; that is what he knows history would look like if he could see it as a whole, which he never can. In point of fact, he can only see it in bits; he can only be acquainted with certain periods, and only competent in very small parts of those periods. It is no blame to Smollett that he dislikes Gothic; he has not had time to study it; that is to say, his civilisation has not had time. Give it time, and it will turn to Gothic and "discover" it, and an infinity of other things too. For humanity studies its history somewhat as Tristram Shandy wrote his life; it takes two years to write the history of a day; but humanity can do what the individual writer cannot, and—subject to the maintenance of life on the planet—pursue the process *ad infinitum*.

At any given moment, therefore, the historian can only present an interim report on the progress of historical studies, and there will be gaps in it. These gaps will appear as breaches in continuity, periods in which the historian loses track of the development. Necessarily, therefore, the history of these gaps will appear an irrational history, a history of muddle and failure and misdirected energies, the history, in a word, of a Dark Age. It may be objected that the gaps ought to appear as mere blanks; not as an irrational history, but as the absence of any history whatever. This would be so, if the historian's ignorance concerning these periods were complete; but in point of fact there are many things, at any given moment in the advance of our knowledge, concerning which we know just enough to make them appear puzzling and unintelligible. This is so in historical studies, as elsewhere. Smollett knew enough about the Middle Ages to know that they had a taste in buildings very different from his own; not enough to see why they had that taste. His condemnation of the Middle Ages as a period of decadence was simply a confession that his own mediaeval studies—or rather, those of his entire generation—were in an unfinished and unsatisfactory condition.

In this condition, we see history split up into disconnected episodes, each episode forming a relatively intelligible whole, separated from its neighbours by dark ages. That is the point of view from which we see history in cycles. Each period with which we are tolerably acquainted, each period which we understand well enough to appreciate the problems and motives of its agents, stands out as something luminous, intelligible, rational, and therefore admirable. But each period is an island of light in a sea of darkness. If we ask why it arose out of barbarism, and why it relapsed into barbarism, we cannot answer; and the reason is that if we knew enough to answer the question we should cease to ask it; for if we knew exactly how the Roman Empire (for instance) declined and fell, what it changed into and how, then the Roman Empire would be to us no longer an island of light in the midst of darkness; the light of our own historical knowledge would have illuminated the Dark Ages and they would no longer appear as dark; we should see that the Roman Empire, instead of simply disappearing, changed; that its outward forms died, while the spirit that had filled them was growing up with unimpaired vigour to find expression in others no less worthy of itself. But so long as we do not know this, so long as we have not yet learnt what the men of the Dark Ages were driving at, we shall necessarily continue to think either that they were driving at nothing or that they were trying to be Romans, and failing. The cyclical view of history is thus a function of the limitations of historical knowledge. Everyone who has any historical knowledge at all sees history in cycles; and those who do not know the cause think that history is really built thus. When they come to settle the exact position and rhythm of the cycles, no two exactly agree; though a certain measure of agreement is found among contemporaries, owing to the fact that the historical knowledge of a given generation, and therefore its historical ignorance, is to a great extent common property. Hence it is easy to believe in a general agreement, and to suppose that the differences of opinion are mere matters of detail[7] which the advance of scientific history will dispel. That belief is a sheer illusion. A comparison of views based on a wider induction, like our comparison between Smollett and Professor Petrie, will show that the divergences go down to rock-bottom. And it thus becomes reasonably certain that further advances in knowledge will not remove the discrepancies but will cause them to reappear in ever fresh places, constantly upsetting the fundamental valuations on which each successive system of cycles was based. Some system of cycles there must always be for every historical student, as every man's shadow must fall somewhere on his own landscape; but as his shadow moves with every movement he makes, so his cyclical view of history will shift and dissolve, decompose and recompose itself anew, with every advance in the historical knowledge of the individual and the race.

[7] Thus Messrs. Goddard and Gibbons (*Civilisation or Civilisations*, 1926) set out confessedly to popularise Spengler, but announce without apparent misgiving that "it is not always possible to accept his interpretations" and in fact modify his scheme to taste.

The Limits of Historical Knowledge*

THE DOUBTFUL STORY of successive events." With this con-
temptuous phrase[1] Bernard Bosanquet brushed aside the
claim of history to be considered a study deserving the attention
of a thoughtful mind. Unsatisfactory in form, because never
rising above uncertainty; unsatisfactory in matter, because always
concerned with the transitory, the successive, the merely particular as opposed to the universal; a chronicle of small beer, and
an untrustworthy chronicle at that. Yet Bosanquet was well read
in history; he had taught it as a young man at Oxford, and his
first published work had been a translation of a recent German
book on the Athenian constitution; he knew that a vast amount
of the world's best genius in the last hundred years had been
devoted to historical studies; and when, late in life, he asked
himself what it came to, that was all he could say.

There are, as I have pointed out, two heads in his indictment
of historical knowledge: that it is doubtful, and that its objects
are transitory. I propose here to consider the first of these alone.
It is by no means an isolated expression of distrust. On the con-

* Reprinted from *Journal of Philosophical Studies* (1928), with the
permission of the editor of *Philosophy* (new title).
[1] *The Principle of Individuality and Value*, p. 78.

trary, we have long been familiar with the idea that history is incapable of arriving at certainty. Epigrams describing it as *une fable convenue,* or the historian's art as *celle de choisir, entre plusieurs mensonges, celui qui ressemble le plus à la vérité,* come back to our minds, and lead them, through eighteenth-century illuminism, back to Descartes, and his polemic against history as a type of thought not susceptible of that mathematical clearness and distinctness which alone reveal the presence of indubitable truth. In fact, this accusation has been a commonplace of European thought for two or three hundred years; and curiously enough, these have been exactly the years during which historical studies have most greatly flourished and produced the most original and unexpected results. One might almost imagine that historical thought, in its most active and successful incarnation, and historical scepticism, doubt as to the value of that thought, were twins, like Brother Date and Brother Dabitur. This at any rate is true, that historical scepticism has not in point of fact been either a cause or a symptom of any decay in historical studies. It follows, either that the human mind is grotesquely illogical (the favourite conclusion of careless observers and indolent thinkers), or else that the function of historical scepticism is not to deny the validity of historical thought, but in some way not fully defined to call attention to its limits.

In order to explore the second alternative (the first is not worth exploring, for if it were true the exploration would be vain) let us consider what case there is to be made out for historical scepticism.

All history is the fruit of a more or less critical and scientific interpretation of evidence. Now there are two loop-holes for scepticism. First, it may be said that the interpretation is never as critical, never as scientific as it might be; that the most learned and most careful historians are able to blunder amazingly in their treatment of evidence, and that therefore we can never be certain that we have interpreted the evidence rightly. But this is a perfectly general topic of scepticism, directed essentially not against history but against all forms of thought; the eternal abstract possibility of this kind of error is identical with the danger that any piece of reckoning or arguing or observing may have been bungled; and consequently this is in no sense a special indictment against historical knowledge.

Secondly, it may be pointed out that the historian, unlike the mathematician or philosopher or biologist, has something to interpret which is called evidence: his documents, his data, his records, or sources. What evidence is there for the binomial theorem? None; the question is meaningless. What evidence is there for Plato's theory of Ideas? Everything is evidence for it, if you believe it; everything evidence against it, if you disbelieve it. In other words, the conception of evidence does not enter into the process of thought by which it is defended or assailed. What evidence is there for or against the inheritance of acquired characteristics? None; what might loosely be called *evidence for* it would be properly described as *well-attested cases of* it. The experiments which corroborate or overthrow a biological theory are not sources or documents, precisely because, if they are impugned, they can be repeated, done over again. You cannot "repeat" Herodotus, or write him over again, if you doubt something that he says; that is what shows him to be, in the strict sense of the word, evidence.

Now—and this is the root of historical scepticism—we only have a strictly limited quantity of evidence concerning any historical question; it is seldom free from grave defects, it is generally tendencious, fragmentary, silent where it ought to be explicit, and detailed where it had better be silent; even at its best, it is never free from these and similar faults, it only refrains from thrusting them indecently upon our notice. Hence the best may be the worst, because it lulls us into a false security and induces us to mistake its incompleteness for completeness, its tendenciousness for sincerity, and to become innocent accomplices in its own deceit. Indeed, the poetic inspiration of Clio the Muse is never more needed, and never more brilliantly employed, than by the task of lulling to sleep the critical faculties of the historical student, while she sings his imagination a Siren's song. But if he binds himself to the mast and refuses to alter his course, he ceases to be a dupe and becomes a sceptic. He will now say, "I know that my evidence is incomplete. I know that I have only an inconsiderable fraction of what I might have had, if fate had been kinder; if the library of Alexandria had survived, if the humanists had been luckier or better supported in their search for manuscripts, if a thousand things had happened which did not happen, I should have had a mass of evidence where now I have only a few shreds. The wholesale destruction of documents due to the French Revolution, and the holocaust of manorial records and title-deeds now going on in England since the passing of Lord Birkenhead's Real Property Act—tempered though it is by the efforts of historical societies and the authority of the Master of the Rolls—have blotted out irreplaceably a vast percentage of the once existing sources for mediaeval history in France and England; what is left will never be more than a fragment, never enough to form the basis for a complete history of the Middle Ages. But even had these catastrophes not happened, our sources, though more extensive, would still be incomplete. We should have more to study, but our results would not really be more certain, except in the doubtful sense in which a larger finite quantity approximates more nearly to infinity."

To say this may seem tantamount to renouncing historical certainty altogether. Yet it must be said. Only by shutting our eyes to the most familiar and obvious facts can we fail to see that the evidence to the whole of which we always appeal when we decide a debated historical point is a mere fragment of what we might have had, if our luck had been better. How vital the Paston Letters are to our knowledge of the fifteenth century; yet it is only by luck that we have them at all, and if our luck had been different we might have had not one such collection but a dozen, giving us on the balance a very different picture of the period. We toil and sweat to get the last ounce of inferential knowledge out of the sources we possess, whereas if we could acquire only a few more, our inferences would be confirmed or overthrown by the merest glance at the new documents. Only actual experience, or, failing that, a careful study of the history of research, can show how utterly the historian is at the mercy of his sources and how completely an addition to his sources may alter his conclusions. No doubt, the scientist may be no less profoundly affected by a new experiment; but this gives him no deep sense of impotence or futility, because it is his business to invent the crucial experiment and his fault if he does not; whereas the historian, however hard he works at the discovery of sources, depends in the long run on the chance that someone did not break up the Monumentum Ancyranum to burn in a lime-kiln, or light the kitchen fire with the Paston Letters.

And this, perhaps, is the real sting of historical scepticism. Doubt is a disease endemic in human thought; if history is doubtful, so is science, so is philosophy; in every department of knowledge, everything is doubtful until it has been satisfactorily settled, and even then it becomes doubtful again unless the doubter can settle it afresh for himself. In mathematics, we are not plagued by the doubtfulness of our theorems, because if we feel unhappy about the axiom of parallels we can think it out on our own account and arrive at an independent opinion; in physics, if we doubt the accepted view about falling bodies, we can climb a tower and test them. But the sources of history we must take or leave. They are not, like scientific or philosophical theorems, results of processes which we can repeat for ourselves; they are results, but results of processes which we cannot repeat; hence they are a solid barrier to thought, a wall of "data" against which all we can do is to build lean-to sheds of inference, not knowing what strains it is capable of bearing. The peculiar, the disastrous doubtfulness of history lies not in the fact that everything in it is dubitable, but in the fact that these doubts cannot be resolved. Everywhere else, it seems, knowledge grows by a healthy oscillation between doubt and certainty: you are allowed to doubt as much as you like, to say, like Hobbes on first looking into Euclid, "By God, it is impossible!" because it is by facing and answering these doubts that you acquire knowledge; but in history we must not doubt; we dare not doubt; we must assume that our evidence is adequate, though we know it to be inadequate, and trustworthy, though we know it to be tainted, for if we did not, our occupation as historians would be gone. The most we can do is to discover and collect, with infinite pains, the extant sources bearing on certain types of problem; to publish vast collections of charters, chronicles, inscriptions, and so forth, whose very bulk overawes the imagination and makes us ashamed to suggest that they may be too small to contain the whole truth even about a little thing. We bolster ourselves up by the ponderous mass of learning at our disposal, when the disease from which we suffer demands not more that is doubtful, but a little, however little, that is certain—a single fact that we can check for ourselves, not an ever-increasing number that we can never check. For what, in history, we call checking a statement is not really checking it at all; it is only comparing one statement with another statement.

This feeling, that in historical studies the mind is bound hand and foot by an act of irrational acquiescence, whereas in science and philosophy it is free to question everything, to reject everything that it cannot substantiate, and assert nothing that it cannot accept on the authority of its own thinking, seems to be what Bosanquet has expressed in the sentence which I quoted at the beginning. Now it is easy to reply that this is hypercriticism; that such doubts do not affect actual historians in the actual course of their work, but only fastidious and probably unsympathetic spectators of that work; and that in point of fact, so far from its being true that history is unable to bear inspection, it is constantly being revised by enormous numbers of intelligent people, who actually all come to very much the same conclusions—that Charles I was beheaded, that Charles II was a ladies' man, that James II fled the country, and so on through a catalogue which may or may not be small beer, but is at least not found doubtful by anyone who takes the trouble to inquire into it.

Such a reply, I must confess, brings a breath of fresh air into an argument which had begun to smell stuffy. It is always with a sense of relief that, after arguing the hind leg off a donkey, one goes out into the field to look at the animal for oneself; and hypercriticism is no doubt the right term for an argument which proves that history, or religion, or politics, is an impossible or idiotic pursuit, when all the time one is aware that plenty of intelligent people are pursuing it in an intelligent spirit. But you cannot dispel an argument by calling it hypercritical. If your donkey has four visible legs, and you can prove that it ought to have three, the discrepancy is a reason not for ceasing to think about the donkey's anatomy, but for thinking about it again: revising, not merely ignoring, the original argument.

It is important to recognise this principle in the interest of all sound philosophical inquiry. People are often tempted to argue thus: "Such and such a view, if pressed home, leads to scepticism. Now scepticism is a self-contradictory position, because it materially claims to possess the knowledge which formally it denies; therefore whatever leads logically to scepticism leads to self-contradiction and is false. This is a sufficient refutation of such and such a view, which accordingly we hereby dismiss from further consideration." This type of refutation, though logically valid, is always unsatisfactory, because it belongs to "eristic," to use Plato's distinction, not to "dialectic." The critic has made a debating point against the view in question, and has left its advocate silenced but unconvinced; aware that his argument has not received justice, but has merely been blugeoned into momentary submission. The bludgeon of a coarse common sense is a very necessary part of the philosopher's armoury; as the truthful man must know how ψεύδη λέγειν ὡς δεῖ so the philosopher must know how to be stupid ὡς δεῖ, and reply to an argument—a perfectly sound argument, it may be—"this is merely an exercise in logical ingenuity; the Facts are, so and so." But if one makes up one's mind to be permanently stupid, as those would have us do who teach their disciples (while reserving other weapons for their own service) the exclusive use of the common-sense bludgeon, one is merely condemning oneself to learn nothing. When you have clubbed the sceptic into silence, get out your scalpel and dissect him; and you may be able to pick his brains to some purpose.

The contentions of historical scepticism—to take up the scalpel—are by no means the mere product of an unintelligent inspection of historical work from the outside. In the preceding paragraphs the writer has stated them altogether as the fruit of his own experience in historical research, and could enlarge on the topic considerably without for a moment ceasing to give an accurate description of that experience in one of its most prominent features. In reading history-books and memorising their contents, and even in teaching history to students, this feature sinks into the background and may be altogether lost to sight. But when one takes up the study of some difficult historical question as yet unsettled, and enters with well-equipped and honest opponents into the *concordia discors* of learned controversy, there is one thing which one cannot fail to observe. This is the existence of what I may call rules of the game. One rule—the first—runs thus: "You must not say anything, however true, for which you cannot produce evidence." The game is won not by the player who can reconstitute what really happened, but by the player who can show that his view of what happened is the one which the evidence accessible to all players, when criticised up to the hilt, supports. Suppose a given view is in fact the correct one, and suppose

(granted it were possible) that all the extant evidence, interpreted with the maximum degree of skill, led to a different
view, no evidence supporting the correct view: in that case the
holder of the correct view would lose the game, the holder of
the other view win it. Not only is this rule accepted by every
player of the game without protest or question, but anyone can
see it to be reasonable. For there is no way of knowing what
view is "correct," except by finding what the evidence, critically
interpreted, proves. A view defined as "correct, but not supported
by the evidence," is a view by definition unknowable, incapable
of being the goal of the historian's search. And at the same time,
every historian actually engaged in such work keenly recognises
the limited character of his sources, and knows very well that it
is no more in his power to add to them than it is in the power of
a chess-player to conjure a third bishop into existence. He must
play the game with the pieces that he has; and if he can find a
new piece—quote a hitherto unexploited source of information
—he must begin a new game, after putting it on the table for his
opponent to use as well as himself. Everyone who has any experience of first-hand historical research, especially in the sharp-
ened form of historical controversy, is thus perfectly familiar
with all the topics of historical scepticism, and is not in the least
perturbed by them. In fact, experience shows that the people who
are scared by them are never the practised historians, who accept
them as a matter of course, but the philosophers of schools committed to theories which they seem, rightly or wrongly, to contradict.

But, I shall be told, I have frankly reduced history to a game.
I have deprived its narratives of all objective value, and degraded
them to a mere exercise in the interpretation of arbitrarily selected bodies of evidence, every such body being selected by the
operation of chance and confessedly impotent to prove the truth.

It is time to drop the metaphor of a game. The so-called rules
of the game are really the definition of what historical thinking

is; the winner of the game is the historian proper—the person who thinks historically, whose thought fulfils the ideal of historical truth. For historical thinking means nothing else than interpreting all the available evidence with the maximum degree of critical skill. It does not mean discovering what really happened, if "what really happened" is anything other than "what the evidence indicates." If there once happened an event concerning which no shred of evidence now survives, that event is not part of any historian's universe; it is no historian's business to discover it; it is no gap in any historian's knowledge that he does not know it. If he had any ideas about it, they would be supernatural revelations, poetic fancies, or unfounded conjectures; they would form no part whatever of his historical thought. "What really happened" in this sense of the phrase is simply the thing in itself, the thing defined as out of all relation to the knower of it, not only unknown but unknowable, not only unknowable but non-existent.

Historical scepticism may now be seen in its proper function, as the negative side of the definition of historical knowledge. There is a permanent tendency in all thought—it is sometimes called the plain man's realism—to think of the object as a "thing in itself," a thing out of all relation to the knowledge of it, a thing existing in itself and by itself. From that point of view, the object of history appears as simply "the past"; the sum total of events that have happened; and the aim of the historian appears as the discovery of the past, the finding out of what has happened. But in the actual practice of historical thinking, the historian discovers that he cannot move a step towards the achievement of this aim without appealing to evidence; and evidence is something present, something now existing, regarded as a relic or trace left by the past. If the past had left no traces, he could never come to know it; and if it has, so to speak, inextricably confused its own traces, all he can do is to disentangle them up to the limit of his own powers. The past simply as past is wholly unknowable; it is the past as residually preserved in the present that is alone knowable. The discovery that the past as such is unknowable is the scepticism which is the permanent and necessary counterpart of the plain man's realism. It is its counterpart, because it asserts the exact opposite; the one asserts that the past as such can be known and is known by history, the other, that it is not known by history and cannot be known. It is a permanent counterpart, because wherever historical thinking is actually done, the discovery which is the basis of historical scepticism is invariably made. Date and Dabitur really are twins. It is a necessary counterpart, because without qualification by historical scepticism, historical realism is wholly false, and must lead to absurd misconceptions of the limits of historical knowledge.

Historical realism by itself implies that whatever is included in the sum total of events that have happened is a possible and legitimate object of historical knowledge: a thing that all historians can and therefore (*qua* historians) ought to know. Every historian as such ought to know the whole past. That being impossible owing to human fraility, the best historian is the one who knows the largest amount of the past; and the more information he can acquire, the better historian he becomes. This leads to countless absurdities. Every historian knows that to be an historian one must be a specialist, and that the historian who tries to know everything knows nothing. But historical realism would imply the reverse. It would imply that historical knowledge is to be reckoned by the quantity of facts with which acquaintance has been scraped, and that the greatest historical writer is the writer of the longest history of the world. Again, every historian knows that there are some questions—pseudoquestions rather—into which it is not his business to inquire, because there is no available evidence towards their answer; and that it is no shame to him to be ignorant by what name Achilles was called when he was disguised as a maiden. But historical realism would imply that this is incorrect; that there are no

limits whatever to historical knowledge except the limits of the
past as past, and that therefore the question what Julius Caesar
had for breakfast the day he overcame the Nervii is as genuinely
historical a problem as the question whether he proposed to become king of Rome. Again, historical realism involves the absurdity of thinking of the past as something still existing by
itself in a νοητὸς τόπος of its own; a world where Galileo's weight
is still falling, where the smoke of Nero's Rome still fills the
intelligible air, and where interglacial man is still laboriously
learning to chip flints. This limbo, where events which have
finished happening still go on, is familiar to us all; it is the room
in the fairy-tale, where all the old moons are kept behind the
door; it is the answer to the poet's refrain: *Mais où sont les neiges
d'antan?* It is the land east of the sun and west of the moon. Its
prose name is Nowhere.

An event that has finished happening is just nothing at all.
It has no existence of any kind whatever. The past is simply non-
existent; and every historian feels this in his dealings with it.
Until he feels it firmly and habitually, his historical technique is
precarious. Realistic philosophers who try to fit him out with a
real past in order to serve as object for his thought greatly mistake his requirements. He does not want a real past; or rather, he
only wants that in his moments of crude realism. In his moments
of scepticism he discovers that he does not possess it, and reflexion shows that he gets along very well without it.

What the historian wants is a real present. He wants a real
world around him (not, of course, a world of things in themselves, unknown and unknowable, but a world of things seen
and heard, felt and described); and he wants to be able to see
this world as the living successor of an unreal, a dead and
perished, past. He wants to reconstruct in his mind the process
by which *his* world—the world in those of its aspects which at
this particular moment impress themselves on *him*—has come to
be what it is. This process is not now going on. The realistic

account of knowledge as apprehension of an independently existing object does not apply to his knowledge of it. It is not existing at all, and he is in no natural sense of the word apprehending
it. If "imagine" is our only term for the "apprehension" of a
non-existent object, he is imagining it; but that will not fit either,
because imagining knows nothing of the difference between truth
and error, and he is doing his best to avoid error and achieve
truth. He is trying to know the past; not the past as it was in
itself—for that is not only non-existent but unknowable into the
bargain—but the past as it appears from its traces in this present:
the past of *his* world, or *his* past, the past which is the proper
object of *his* historical researches, specialised as all historical researches must be, and arising directly out of the world he perceives around him, as all historical researches must arise.

From this point of view many problems concerning the proper
aims, methods, and objects of historical thought find their solution. This is not the place to demonstrate the truth of that claim;
I hope to do it in detail elsewhere. It is enough for the present to
have stated the general thesis that all historical thought is the
historical interpretation of the present; that its central question
is: "How has this world as it now exists come to be what it is?"
and that for this reason the past concerns the historian only so
far as it has led to the present. By leading to the present, it has
left its traces upon the present; and by doing that, it has supplied
the historian with evidence concerning itself, a starting-point for
his investigations. The historian does not first think of a problem
and then search for evidence bearing on it; it is his possession of
evidence bearing on a problem that alone makes the problem a
real one.

It thus appears that history is not doubtful at all. It seemed
doubtful, to say the least, so long as we imagined its object to be
the past as past; but though the question "what really happened,"
where "what happened," and "what the evidence proves" are
assumed as distinct, is necessarily doubtful, the question "what

the evidence proves" is not doubtful. Granted a training in historical methods, and equipment of historical scholarship, without which no one can fairly judge,[2] it is possible to take a particular problem, to study the solution of that problem advanced by a particular historian on a particular review of the evidence, and within the limits of this problem, as stated, to raise the question whether he has or has not proved his case. That question can be answered, by a competent scholar, with no more doubt than must attend any man's answer to any question that can be asked in any department of knowledge. And in the certainty of that answer lies the formal dignity, the logical worth, the scientific value in the highest sense of that word, of historical studies.

[2] It may be worth while to point out that even a rigidly cogent historical argument always seems to contain loop-holes of doubt, to a critic unfamiliar with the matter in hand; a reader, e.g., who does not know enough numismatics to know what the possible alternatives in a given case are, cannot judge the solidity of an expert numismatist's discussion of that case, because he will see that certain alternatives are tacitly ruled out, without knowing why. Had the numismatist been writing for beginners, he ought to have explained why; not otherwise. One might have supposed that the logic of an historical argument could be judged by one ignorant of its subject-matter; that is not the case. But I must not enlarge on this here.

A Philosophy of Progress*

W HETHER THE WORLD has become a better place to live in seems at first sight a straightforward kind of question—a question, one might suppose, of facts. We know something about human life as it is lived today, and something about it as it has been lived in the past;[1] whether it has improved or deteriorated, then, seems capable of being settled by a simple comparison.

Two notable attempts at settling the question have been made. The ancient Greeks and Romans were interested in it, and on the whole they answered it in a fairly definite manner. Human life, they said, had once been a very fine thing, but it had deteriorated; history had consisted of a succession of ages each worse than the last, and if one looked forward one could only look forward to

* Reprinted from *The Realist* (1929), with the permission of Macmillan & Co. Ltd.

[1] As my title indicates, the subject of these pages is the light thrown on the problem of progress by the facts of recorded human history. Within the limits of a short essay it would be impossible to deal also with the relation between the conception of progress and that of evolution. To separate the two subjects is possible because a careful scrutiny of historical records shows no such alteration in human faculties, within historical times, as would compel the historian to take into account an evolution of human faculties, presumably accompanying an evolution of the human brain, during these times.

disaster. The question was raised again by European thinkers of the eighteenth and nineteenth centuries; and they too answered it, on the whole, in a definite manner, but in the opposite sense. Human life, they said, had progressed from humble origins to a splendid maturity; and there was no reason why it should not continue to advance in the same direction.

It might be supposed that, the question being one of mere fact, both were right. The Graeco-Roman world, one might suppose, was really decadent, and the world of the eighteenth and nineteenth centuries really progressive. That this is the correct view seems to be taken for granted by most modern historians. Yet it does not solve the problem. The modern theory of progress, in its complete form, committed itself to the doctrine that progress had been maintained throughout recorded time; and therefore it was logically bound to contradict the ancients' views about the tendency of their own age, and to assert that this had been one of progress, although, at the time, it had seemed one of degeneration. On this point ancients and moderns were at one: whether the world was getting better or worse, it was doing so, they thought, in obedience to a law.

But why should not the law, instead of dictating a simple upward or downward course, dictate an alternation of the two? A series of waves, each rising to a crest and falling into a trough before the next rise? And why should not the wave-summits lie on an ascending or descending line, or even on a line itself alternating between upward and downward tendencies?

The real objection to this—the so-called theory of historical cycles—is that it attempts, like the old Ptolemaic[2] astronomy, to

[2] The theory of cycles is Ptolemaic; the theory that from the point of view of the present day history is a progress is Copernican; and the latter is the theory advanced in this essay. If anyone replies that a thoroughgoing relativism would reconcile the two, I reply, by all means. Once you have accepted the ideas outlined below, you can see cycles of alternate advance and decay wherever you look for them; only you now know that they are relative to your point of view.

meet objections by adding complications, and thereby loses the only merit it had—simplicity. The theory of progress and the theory of decadence are at any rate simple. If anyone says that once, long ago, there was a Golden Age, and we have lost it, and things are getting worse and worse, and one day they will become impossible—well, we at least have some idea what he means. And if someone else says that, on the contrary, things are looking up and we are a great deal better off than we were, and if we go on like this we shall practically annihilate space and time, conquer disease, abolish poverty, and arrive at the millennium— then, once more, we can see what he is driving at, and to some extent sympathise with him. Each point of view, taken at its face value, has something to be said for it, and always had. There has never been any time in the world's history when there was not some case to be made out for the pessimist's cry that the country, or the age, is going to the dogs. And there has never been any time when there was not some case for the optimist's belief that things are improving.

It is necessary to insist on this, because it is easy to be deceived by the general prevalence of an accepted point of view, and to lose sight of a persistent under-current of views opposed to it. Certainly the ancients, in their official pronouncements, as it were, had a tendency to state what I have called the theory of decadence. But when they forgot their orthodox theory of history and allowed themselves simply to comment on contemporary happenings, they constantly detected in details that very upward movement which, in general, they denied. Virgil's song of welcome to the new age of peace and prosperity is not an isolated utterance. Horace is often quoted as the poet-laureate of ancient pessimism:

> Damnosa quid non imminuit dies?
> Ætas parentum, peior avis, tulit
> Nos nequiores, mox daturos
> Progeniem vitiosiorem.

Yet the very ode-sequence which contains these lines of regret
and foreboding is inspired, as a whole, by the same hopes that
inspired Virgil's fourth Eclogue; and next before the poem I
have quoted stands the great "Regulus" ode that begins:

> Cælo tonantem credidimus Iovem
> Regnare; præsens Divus habebitur
> Augustus, adiectis Britannis
> Imperio, gravibusque Persis.

This expectation of a glorious future became a habit with the
Romans, so that even in the darkest years of imperial history we
come across coins with legends describing the reigning Emperor
as "Restitutor Reipublicae" or "Liberator Orbis," and acclaim-
ing "Pax Perpetua" or "Felicium Temporum Reparatio"—a
legend whose popularity is evident from its constant reappear-
ance. The Romans might think that the Golden Age was past,
but they constantly caught themselves thinking that it was in the
near future too.

This tendency is not confined to the Romans. If Hesiod de-
plores the progressive harshness of the ages, the Homeric hero
retorts, "We boast that we are better than our fathers"; if Plato
finds it natural to classify the varieties of political constitution in
the form of a series of progressive perversions, Aristotle, writing
the history of philosophy, presents it without hesitation or apology as the history of an upward movement.

If we turn to the eighteenth and nineteenth centuries, we shall
very soon find the same thing happening. Progress is now the
orthodox creed; but there have never been wanting dissentients.
Jean-Jacques Rousseau thought that civilisation was a mistake,
and his view was shared, in a more or less qualified form, by a
good many people. The central nineteenth century, the generation that witnessed the triumph of the idea of progress, witnessed
also a determined guerilla warfare against that idea, carried on
by men like Schopenhauer, Carlyle, Ruskin, Matthew Arnold,

Nietzsche, whose main object in life was to show up the weaknesses, vices, follies, and Philistinisms of the age and undermine its complacent self-approval. And if we take Tennyson as the modern counterpart of Horace, the poet-laureate of progress, we can place, side by side with the optimism of "Locksley Hall," the fierce revolt of "Maud":

Peace sitting under her olive, and slurring the days gone by,
When the poor are hovell'd and hustled together, each sex, like swine,
When only the ledger lives, and when only not all men lie;
Peace in her vineyard—yes!—but a company forges the wine.

And the vitriol madness flushes up in the ruffian's head,
Till the filthy by-lane rings to the yell of the trampled wife,
And chalk and alum and plaster are sold to the poor for bread,
And the spirit of murder works in the very means of life. . . .

These are the reflections of Queen Victoria's laureate, the favourite of the age that made the idea of progress its own, on the "blessings of Peace," the "days of advance, the works of the men of mind."

In the past, then, people have not found it so simple to decide whether the world has become a better or worse place to live in. An easy-going popular philosophy, sceptical about the possibility of settling such questions, will suggest that optimism and pessimism are functions of the digestive system—a dogma which would hardly bear the light of inquiry into the question whether William Morris's digestion was worse than Herbert Spencer's—or, more penetratingly, will define a pessimist as a person who has to live with an optimist. The value of these suggestions is that they direct our attention away from the facts of history and towards the disposition with which people envisage those facts. They suggest that progress and decadence are not matters of fact at all, but habits of mind, ways of looking at things, matters of temperament.

Taken literally, that suggestion would be merely cynical. But

none the less it may serve a useful turn. You cannot live on
cynicism, any more than you can live on salt; but woe to the man
who tries to live without it! Let us develop the suggestion and see
how much of it proves acceptable.

Whether you think the course of events is an upward or a
downward course depends not on *it* but on *you*. It is a matter of
taste. It depends on what sort of things you like. If you like
pottering about the roads and listening to the birds, you will
regret the motor-car. If you enjoy the fat rotundity of Norman
architecture, you will deplore the leanness of Gothic. But con-
versely, you may like being able to travel fast and cheaply; or
you may think Norman clumsy and Gothic graceful. And in that
case, of course, you will think these changes are changes for the
better.

This is a cynical view of the case because it implies that our
preferences are mere matters of chance or caprice. And, in order
to recommend his theory of the unreasonableness of mankind,
the cynic has perverted his facts. It is not the whole truth that
some people like pottering about the roads and others like rush-
ing along them. Some people like both. I am one of them; and I
like motor-cars when I am in one, and dislike them when I am
not. But if I ask myself whether I prefer to be able to potter
about the roads, or to be able to rush along them, recognising, as
I must if I think about it, that I can't have it both ways, then I
shall probably answer, "I am sorry to give up the good old
English habit of using the roads to potter about on; but if it
comes to a choice, give me motor-cars with all that they imply."

Again, take the case of Norman and Gothic building, which is
instructive just because we are apt to think that preferences in
aesthetic matters are mere questions of caprice. The reason why
people stopped building Norman and began building Gothic
was an engineering reason. They wanted a more favourable ratio
of strength to weight; and they found that they could get it by
substituting a compact shaft for a thick pier whose bulk consisted

largely of loose rubbish, and by lifting the crowns of their vaults into a point. The sense of slenderness or lightness or grace which we have in looking at Gothic buildings is our tribute to this new and more efficient strength-weight ratio.

Why, then, should anyone prefer Norman to Gothic? Simply because Gothic is, so to speak, too clever for him. It raises the strength-weight ratio to a figure which he feels impossible and finds unconvincing. He feels that more bulk of stone is wanted to secure the stability of the structure. Therefore he finds the Norman style more comfortable, as it were, because of the obvious adequacy of the materials to the work they have to do. The result is that though he may admire Gothic he feels safer with Norman.

Now, the view we are considering is that whether you think the course of events is an upward or downward course depends not on *it* but on *you*. How does this apply to the transition from Norman to Gothic?

That transition was definitely an improvement, if you judge it by the standard of engineering. The main purpose of the architect is to build; the Gothic architect built stronger and cheaper than the Norman. Incidentally he produced buildings with lighter interiors, and improved them in a good many other points of detail. But what of the building as a work of art? Is Gothic more *beautiful* than Norman? To this, one person will reply, "Yes; it is more beautiful because of its new grace, its soaring lines, its buoyancy, its flame-like or flower-like defiance of mere weight." Another will reply, "No; it is less beautiful, because it has lost that visible and expressive solidity which reveals to us, in a Norman building, the earthiness and stoniness of the material and the massiveness of the edifice."

Both are right; only it is not a question of more and less. In the change from Norman to Gothic we have lost one beauty and gained another, just as we lost the pleasure of pottering about the roads and gained the pleasure of driving along them. Every phase of art has its own beauty, which it is idle to assess in terms of a scale of degrees; to do that is simply to fall a victim to the pedagogue's habit of marking everything as if it were an examination paper.

The connoisseur of architecture, therefore, is merely confessing his own personal limitations if he says that he likes Gothic for its slenderness and dislikes Norman for its fatness, or *vice versa*. He ought to like Gothic for its slenderness and like Norman for its fatness. He ought to enjoy Salisbury spire because it soars; he ought to enjoy Durham because it does not soar, but stands, square and stout, on its rock; he ought to enjoy the dome of the Pantheon, as you see it from Janiculum, because it neither soars nor stands, but squats like some monstrous prehistoric tortoise among the roofs of Rome. But this catholicity of taste, which is the goal of all true taste, would not in any way prevent him from recognising the logical and rational character of the development from Roman to Romanesque and from Romanesque to Gothic. And this he must recognise if he studies its history.

A history in which every change occurs for a sufficient reason may or may not deserve the name of progress; but at any rate it is not a tale told by an idiot, full of sound and fury, signifying nothing. It is a story with a plot, the intelligible story of the doings of intelligent people.

The chief cause for the spread of the idea of progress in the eighteenth and nineteenth centuries was the development of historical studies. The growth of historical science in the eighteenth century was not less remarkable, and not less influential, than the growth of physical science in the seventeenth. And when people began to reap the fruit of these historical studies, when the picture of history as a whole began to take shape before their eyes, a startling discovery burst upon them: *it made sense*. It had a plot. It revealed itself as something coherent, significant, intelligible.

It was a genuine discovery. It was true, and it remains true, that history lacks plot or significance only when it is told by an idiot. As we have seen, the history of architecture is a history of inventions by which the technique of building has been developed from point to point for centuries together. Told by an idiot, the history of architecture would become a meaningless succession of whims and fashions. Told by a competent person, it has a plot; the various changes which it records are rational changes. The same is true of any other piece of history.

This is illustrated in a striking way by a critical phase in the development of the idea of progress. In the eighteenth century it was generally held that progress, though a reality since the Renaissance, had not been continuous in the past, because the Middle Ages had been a period of darkness and barbarism, a real decline from the Graeco-Roman age. This view was closely connected with the theory of eighteenth-century *philosophes* that religion was a kind of illusion imposed by wily priests, for their own nefarious ends, on a credulous people. The Romantic movement discovered that religion was a permanent and necessary function of human life, and at the same time began trying to find out something about the Middle Ages, a subject till then practically untouched by the advance of historical inquiry. As always, a deeper study brought with it a more sympathetic understanding; and it was soon realised that the Middle Ages were not a period of darkness and barbarism after all, but a period of remarkable progress and achievement. This discovery was crucial for the theory of progress; for it was now possible to say that the whole of recorded history revealed an unbroken development; and it was this that enabled the theory of progress to arrive at maturity and sweep in triumph over every quarter of European thought.

History, then, has a plot; but is it therefore a progress? The plot of a drama may be a tragic plot. May not the plot of history be tragic too?

If the question is whether history has a "happy ending" or an "unhappy" one, it is not an admissible question. We can tell the story down to the present time, but it is a serial story of which new instalments are always coming out, and whose end we cannot reasonably expect to see. Apocalyptic revelations of this end have been claimed by various religious and political creeds, whose votaries have been privileged to see an advance number of the concluding instalment; but these visions are denied to the historian, and in these pages we are not concerned with them. For us, history can reconstruct—within very definite limits—the past. Study of our own surroundings can reveal, again within definite limits, the present. The future is hidden. Or rather, there is nothing to hide, for it does not yet exist; it is unknowable for the good reason that it has not happened. For us, therefore, it is idle to ask whether the ending of history, when it comes, will be a happy or an unhappy one.

But we may at least be asked whether the course of history down to the present has been for good or for evil. Has the sum of human happiness increased or decreased in the past?

The answer is that we cannot tell, because the question is meaningless. Happiness, if it consists of feelings of pleasure and pain, cannot be summed. Hedonism, grotesquely imagining that pleasure and pain could be handled by the methods of bookkeeping, spoke of adding up pleasures, subtracting the sum of pains, and so arriving at a figure for all the world like an income-tax return. No hedonist ever gave an example of this extraordinary feat; but five minutes' honest attempt to perform it will convince anybody that it cannot be done except in a purely arbitrary way. You can, certainly, attach numerical "values" to pleasures and pains, and operate with the numbers so obtained; by this method you can prove that twenty glasses of port will give you twenty times as much pleasure as one glass, or that a day with 100 units of pleasure and 99 units of pain is indistinguishable in hedonic value from a day with 1 unit of pleasure and 0 units of pain, and other equally profound psychological truths. But if you have the sense to reject this kind of drivel, and still hanker after the idea of a "sum of human happiness," what meaning can you attach to the word *sum?* What is a sum which cannot be reached by a process of computation?

The sum of human happiness has neither increased, nor diminished, nor remained constant, because there is no such thing. It is easy to select a certain group of desires and to say, "I call an age in which these desires are satisfied happier than an age in which they are not"; but no selection will stand the test of honest criticism. The desires to speak your mind freely, to enlarge your knowledge, to take part in the direction of the common life, are characteristic of modern European man, and he thinks any age unhappy in which freedom in thought and political life are in defect. But it is precisely the having these desires in an acute and persistent shape that makes modern European man what he is, and inspires him with a determination to satisfy them. Men of other ages—the vast majority of men—would consider such desires morbid and exceptional, and find their happiness in being told authoritatively what to think and what to do. Different ages find happiness in different things.

This was the error of the eighteenth-century theory of progress. It was based on a hedonistic philosophy and a staggering self-complacency. The eighteenth-century Frenchmen who invented it thought that the pleasantness of the life of any particular man varied, had always varied, and always would vary, in direct proportion to his resemblance to an eighteenth-century Frenchman. Consequently the past, at any rate since the Renaissance, had been a period of progress because it had gradually evolved the eighteenth-century Frenchman; and all that was left to the future was to bring the rest of the world into conformity with this pattern. What he failed to realize was, that different people might legitimately have different ideas as to what they would like to be; and that Pericles probably got quite as much enjoyment out of being an Athenian as Monsieur Chose got out of being a Parisian.

Can we hold, then, that men have grown better? Does the course of history show an improvement in morals?

That this is so was the opinion of the nineteenth-century believers in progress. They saw through hedonism and realised the futility of judging everything in terms of pleasure; but they flattered themselves (for they, too, had their share of self-complacency) that they were more virtuous, better-mannered, more humane and conscientious, than the men of earlier ages, and they thought that it was this quality in them that past history had laboured to evolve.

The nineteenth century did well to pride itself on having abolished slavery and conceived the idea of universal liberty and brotherhood. It did well to pride itself on its advances in science and humanity. For that matter, the Frenchman of the *grand siècle* had his own very good reasons for pride. But it did not grasp the difference between being humane and being moral. Cruelty is a vice; but so is priggishness; and the self-complacency of the nineteenth century, being based on a high opinion of its own virtue, led it to wallow in the vice of priggishness. The eighteenth century said, "How happy we are!" and laughed until its voice cracked. The nineteenth century said, "How good we are!" and its voice rang false.

Goodness, like beauty and happiness, is not a product of civilisation. A man's moral worth depends not on his circumstances, but on the way in which he confronts them. It was a good act to abolish slavery, but the men who are born into a slaveless world are not automatically made good men by that fact. All it can do for them is to confront them with moral problems of a new kind. This the nineteenth-century believers in progress failed to see. They thought that external circumstances, by being better, made men better. You might as well say that we are better soldiers than Napoleon because our guns have a longer range, or better musicians than Bach because our orchestras are larger. To say this would be foolish, but not more foolish than to condemn as immoral Octavian's prescriptions or the massacres of an Assyrian conqueror, the tortures of mediaeval justice, or the treacheries of Renaissance statecraft, without understanding the circumstances in which they were deliberately embarked upon.

But if the course of history does not show an increase of happiness or an increase of goodness, in what sense, if any, is it a progress?

In order to answer this question, let us return to one of the examples we have already discussed. The history of architecture presents us with a process of development in which each new change has brought the process nearer to the point at which it stands today.

A development is a progress when it is a development into something better. Now we have seen that there can be no increase of beauty or happiness or goodness. But though the buildings of one age are not more beautiful than those of another—since each has its own proper beauty, not to be assessed in terms of any other —the aesthetic problem of any age's architecture is unique: that is to say, a particular age has the task of realising beauty in a particular way. We, for example, have invented reinforced concrete, and our task is to discover how to make it beautiful. We shall not do it by pretending that reinforced concrete is stone or timber; for it is a material with a very decided nature of its own, and we shall only build beautifully in it by understanding this nature and expressing it in our designs. That is the problem of modern architecture.

This problem has a history. It arose in a certain way, at a certain time, and linked itself up with certain events in the past from which it is descended by a kind of genealogy. The problem how to use reinforced concrete has come down to us conditioned by the Greek use of the horizontal architrave, the Roman employment of concrete, the mediaeval method of distributing strains over a skeleton of ribs and buttresses, and so forth. Now the result of this fact is that, if and when we devise a new and beautiful system of reinforced concrete architecture, we shall be able to say that this new architecture is the final outcome of all architectual history. Final, in the sense that it is the last thing *hitherto* produced by that history: that history will cease here nobody supposes, but how it will go on nobody knows.

But—now comes the difficulty—why should we say that our new architecture is better than any of its predecessors? The answer is simple. If we do not think it better, why do we build it? We could easily reproduce Egyptian or Greek or Roman or mediaeval work; why don't we? For it is a curious fact that we do not reproduce ancient buildings, and no one ever has done so. Even Renaissance builders did not attempt to reproduce the antique, they only borrowed features from the antique, to incorporate them in structures whose general principles were far removed from those of ancient buildings. But it would be very easy to reproduce ancient buildings if we wanted to do it. Our reproductions would not have the spontaneity of the originals, but very few people are so sensitive to architectural form as to discover that. Any architect's clerk could produce so accurate a copy of the Parthenon as to deceive ninety-nine aesthetes out of a hundred. But he could not sell it—except, perhaps, fraudulently, to one of the ninety-nine. Our own architecture is the only one that suits our purposes; and therefore it is the only one that is of any value to us, the only one presenting an aesthetic problem which, for us, there is any merit in solving. We do not want to compete with Egypt in building pyramids or with Greece in building peripteral marble temples; but why not? Not because we think these things cannot be well done, but because we do not want to do them. To be perfectly frank, we think it a waste of time to do them. We do not regret our lost power of building pyramids; we think we can employ ourselves, as architects, to better advantage. That is not a condemnation of the ancient Egyptians. We, in their place, should have done likewise, and well for us if we could have made such a fine job of it. But it is not merely a question of Egyptian architecture being best for ancient Egyptians and ours best for ourselves. Our purposes are not something wholly new; they are the ancient immemorial purposes for which man has always erected buildings, and if we refuse to build like the ancients this is not because we think our way of building is better for *us* merely, but because we think it better for mankind.

Or let us glance at another aspect of history—the history of politics. Primitive man, whom the romanticism of a past generation conceived as living in enviable freedom, really lived and lives encased in an iron shell of custom. His customs do not, as a whole, make him unhappy. Sometimes they call upon him for hard sacrifices; so do ours; and, sacrifice for sacrifice, there is little to choose between us. The tendency of modern times to regard the savage's life as necessarily miserable is merely an exaggerated reaction against the old tendency to regard it as necessarily happy. On the whole the savage likes being hide-bound by custom; it gives him more labour in some ways, but in others it saves him just the kind of labour that is really most laborious—the labour of altering age-long habits of mind. He would rather stop at the end of every row to sharpen his soft iron hoe than use a steel hoe which does not get blunt, because it seems unnatural and makes him uncomfortable if his hoe does not get blunt in the proper way. And the same psychological conditions hold good in his political life.

The political system of primitive man is the only system really suited to his psychological structure; in fact it simply *is* that structure expressing itself in terms of politics. Now the development of political life down to the present day has undeniably been a progress in the sense that it has led to the creation of political systems more supple, more adaptable, more responsive to individual initiative from within, and to alterations of conditions without, than the systems of the past. This progress has been achieved by way of a succession of inventions no less definite than the invention of the vault or the invention of the automatic valve for a steam-engine. The inventions whose history is the history of political life have, in a sense, progressively liberated the individual from the tyranny of custom and the crippling weight of a rigid political system; but that way of putting it may easily be exaggerated. Savages would think *our* political systems and social customs quite as oppressive and inimical to happiness as we think theirs. The fact is, we have developed social and political institutions that suit *our* psychological structure, and give scope to those things in us which we consider the most important. If we pride ourselves on being less conventional than savages, we ought to remember that being unconventional is our way of being conventional; our customs themselves permit us to defy them in certain limited ways, and thus our individual freedom of movement is not a real defiance of the customary order of things, but is our way of maintaining that order. By bearing this in mind we can avoid a serious mistake which, unless we escape it, must destroy our power of understanding social and political history. The mistake is to consider progress in these respects as a diminution of the power of society and a corresponding increase in the power—the freedom, the judgment, the responsibility—of the individual. The mistake is strictly a philosophical mistake, which has found its way, through Herbert Spencer, into the social sciences and is doing a good deal to impede a clear sight of the relation between civilised and uncivilised life. The correction of the mistake lies in the realisation that any increase in freedom, intelligence, and self-reliance in individuals is automatically reflected in society, which is not a mythical superhuman being but just individuals themselves in their mutual relations. As the individual gains in power, his social and political life gains in power too; for the rigidity of a primitive political system is not strength but weakness.

The increase in the power of political institutions, which sometimes makes people fear for individual liberty, is thus one of the most certain proofs of human progress, and is both the effect and the cause of an increase in individual liberty itself. Our political institutions are quite unsuited to primitive man, or to ancient Greeks, or to mediaeval barons, or even to the men of the eighteenth century; but they are the best for us, and they have been evolved through a process in the course of which they have incorporated into themselves portions of primitive law, of the Greek city-state, of Roman imperialism, of feudal organisation, and so forth. All these elements have gone to make modern political life what it is; and in so far as modern political life is based on the values which we consider the most important, this evolution must, to us, appear as a progress.

The question whether, on the whole, history shows a progress can be answered, as we now see, by asking another question. Have you the courage of your convictions? If you have, if you regard the things which you are doing as things worth doing, then the course of history which has led to the doing of them is justified by its results, and its movement is a movement forward.

The Philosophy of History*

I. THE IDEA OF A PHILOSOPHY OF HISTORY

1. "Philosophy"

PHILOSOPHY IS THINKING about the world as a whole. To study the nature of selected parts of the world is to be a scientist; to study its nature as a whole is to be a philosopher. Thus, it is the business of one kind of scientist—the mathematical physicist—to study matter and motion; but if anyone says that matter and motion are the only things that exist, he is talking not physics but philosophy. The biologist studies organisms; but Professor Whitehead, when he says that the world is an organism (*Process and Reality,* 1929), is being a philosopher, not a biologist.

In more technical and accurate language, philosophy studies the universal and necessary characteristics of things: science their particular and contingent characteristics. An embryologist studies an egg, but only a few of its characteristics, not all of them; a geometrician, looking at the same egg, will study others; a philosopher, others again. The geometrician studies its shape, and shape is an attribute possessed by many things, but not by all; it

---

* Historical Association Leaflet No. 79 (1930). Reprinted with the permission of The Historical Association.

is therefore a particular, not a universal, characteristic of things. The embryologist studies certain attributes which the egg shares with other organisms in the early stages of their life, and these, too, are particular, not universal, attributes. The philosopher studies such attributes as its unity, its existence, its substantiality; these attributes it shares with all other things whatever.

2. *"Of"*

The philosopher uses the egg as an instance of unity and so forth, but unity might be exemplified equally well by a stone or an ink-pot. Therefore, although the philosopher may talk about eggs, there is no philosophy of eggs, just as there is no geometry of eggs, no arithmetic of pebbles, and no hydrostatics of China tea. When we speak of the philosophy of art, the philosophy of religion, the philosophy of history, and so forth, either we are abusing language and confusing our minds, or else we are suggesting that art or religion or history is somehow a universal and necessary characteristic of things, not merely a particular and contingent characteristic of a certain group of things.

If the philosophy of art is the study of certain things called works of art, and of the minds of certain people called artists, then it studies only a selected part of the world, not the world as a whole; it is a science, not philosophy; and its methods ought to conform to the model of scientific (in this case psychological) research, not that of philosophical thinking. If it is to be a branch of philosophy, it must be able to show that, in the sense in which it uses the word art, every work is a work of art, locomotives and business letters no less than statues and sonnets; it must even show that natural objects are *objets d'art*, and that every man is an artist.

"The philosophy of something" is a legitimate phrase only when the "something" in question is no mere fragment of the world, but is an aspect of the world as a whole—a universal and necessary characteristic of things.

3. *"History"*

If history is the name for a special group of things (such as "past politics" or the like) on the one hand, and for a special group of thoughts on the other, the thoughts which occupy the time and attention of a special group of people called historians, then there is no philosophy of history. History, in that case, is a trade like plumbing or an amusement like horse-racing, and there is no such thing as a philosophy of plumbing or a philosophy of horse-racing. The plumber and the racing man do not find themselves confronted with special philosophical problems which they have to solve on pain of disaster; and the philosopher does not find the plumber or the racing man pregnant with philosophical truths that he cannot learn from another source.

If there is to be a philosophy of history, history must be something more than a trade or an amusement. It must be a universal and necessary human interest, the interest in a universal and necessary aspect of the world. Historians must live, and therefore history must be a trade; but unless history were a universal and necessary human interest the historian's trade would be of less value than the plumber's, because, whereas we pay plumbers to save us having to do our own plumbing, we pay historians to help us to become historians ourselves.

When we think of history as merely a trade or profession, a craft or a calling, we find it hard to justify our existence as historians. What can the historian do for people except turn them into historians like himself? And what is the good of doing that? Is it not simply a vicious circle, whose tendency is to overcrowd the ranks of the profession and to produce an underpaid "intellectual proletariate" of sweated teachers? This may be a valid argument against the multiplication of historians, if history is merely a profession, but it cannot be if history is a universal human interest; for in that case there are already as many historians as there are human beings, and the question is not "Shall

I be an historian or not?" but, "How good an historian shall I be?"

4. History and the Philosophy of History

The question, then, is whether history is a mere trade or craft, or whether it is a universal human interest.

History is the study of the past; to be an historian is to know how things have come to be what they are. But everything has a past; everything has somehow come to be what it is; and therefore the historical aspect of things is a universal and necessary aspect of them. Hence, too, anyone who is interested in anything at all is interested in something that has an historical aspect, and if he is really interested in the thing he must be to some extent interested in this aspect of it. History, as the study of the past, is therefore a universal and necessary human interest—interesting to anybody who is interested in anything—and not the affair of a special professional group.

But history is not only an interest, it is a special kind of interest; an intellectual interest; a form of knowledge. The business of the philosophy of history is to discover the essential characteristics of this form of knowledge. Now, the essential characteristics of any form of knowledge begin to emerge into daylight only when the knowledge in question begins to take shape as a body of thought organised according to its own proper laws and recognised as forming a special field of study. To know who played centre-forward for Aston Villa last year is just as much historical knowledge as to know who won the battle of Cannae; but the essential characteristics of historical knowledge are, on the whole, less clearly exemplified in picking up information from cigarette-cards than in reading Livy, because in the latter case historical knowledge is an end pursued in a sustained and systematic way, by means of a technique consciously adapted to it, whereas in the former it is something casually acquired by a mind whose main interest at the moment lies elsewhere, perhaps in betting on football or in enlarging one's collection of cigarette-cards.

It is, therefore, natural that the philosophy of history should follow a course of development parallel to that of history itself. Where historical knowledge exists only in a desultory and casual form, there will be only a very crude and shallow philosophy of history. Where historical knowledge is a highly-organised thing, involving a technique of its own and a consciousness of its own peculiar aims and methods, the philosophy of history will be a definite and individual philosophical science, whose importance in philosophy as a whole will more or less correspond to the importance of history in human thought as a whole.

With this clue we can turn to the past and describe the way in which the philosophy of history has developed *pari passu* with the development of history itself.

II. HISTORY OF THE IDEA

1. The First Stage: Bacon

For our purpose it is not necessary to go back beyond the seventeenth century. Understanding the phrase "philosophy of history" as we do, we cannot be expected to find philosophies of history in St. Augustine or Hesiod or Amos. These men had the idea of history as proceeding according to some divine or destined plan, but it is only by a confusion of thought that such a plan can be called a philosophy of history. Hesiod's statement that the world has passed through a series of ages, golden, silver, bronze, and iron, was intended for a simple statement of fact. The fact (assuming that it was a fact) was a fact of a very broad and sweeping kind; but a fact of this kind is still a fact, and the statement of it is history and not philosophy. It is wholly for the historian to decide whether the facts were as Hesiod states them or not. As for the Hebrew prophets' reflexions on the history of

their people, the attitude which they express is not that of philosophical thought but that of religious faith.

Before there can be a philosophy of history there must be a
sustained and systematic attempt to build up a body of historical
knowledge. It would, therefore, be more reasonable to look for a
philosophy of history in Herodotus or Thucydides, Polybius or
Livy or Tacitus. But even here we find nothing that can properly
be so called; all that we find is statements of fact, even when
these are broad and sweeping in their scope, like Polybius's picture of Rome standing in the centre of universal history. After
all, the philosophy of history is nothing but the deliberate attempt
to answer the question "what *is* history?" and none of the ancient
historians raised the question. There are hints of it here and there
in the ancient philosophers, but it would be pedantic to reconstruct Artistotle's philosophy of history, or to infer that he
had one, from such remarks as that "poetry is more philosophical
than history" because poetry tells us what such and such a kind of
man would always do, while history tells us what Alcibiades
actually did (*Poetics,* ch. 9).

In Bacon (1561–1626) we do find an attempt to answer the
question "what is history?" Bacon sets before us a systematic
picture of the activities of the human mind, which are three in
number: poetry, history, and philosophy, depending on the three
faculties of imagination, memory, and understanding. His theory
of history is quite simple: historical knowledge is at bottom
simply remembering, and what we cannot remember we must
take on authority from those who do or did. Memory and authority thus form the double root of all history.

Such a theory was well enough at the beginning of the seventeenth century, when, as a matter of fact, historians had hardly
learnt to do more than take on trust whatever statements they
found in their "authorities." But even in Bacon's time it was inadequate; Bacon himself, in his *History of the Reign of King
Henry VII,* did more than he here allows for. Any historian must

work up the materials, which his authorities provide, into a whole; mere transcriptions of sources is not history. The historian must compress and expand, infer steps in the narrative which his sources do not mention, and leave out things which he considers irrelevant or trivial, even though his sources contain them. But these may be dismissed as minor details, or even as things pertaining not to history but rather to the writing of history, until they are brought into light by a development of historical technique which was far beyond the horizon of Bacon.

2. The Problem of Method: Vico

Italy, which since the end of the Middle Ages had led European thought, took the first step away from the crude Baconian philosophy of history. Giambattista Vico (1668–1744), who was at once a philosopher and an historian, laid the foundations of the modern philosophy of history in much the same sense in which Descartes, philosopher and scientist, laid those of the modern philosophy of science. Vico's chosen field, as an historian, was the history of remote antiquity. He studied distant and obscure periods precisely because they were distant and obscure; for his real interest was in historical method, and, according as the sources are scanty and dubious and the subject-matter strange and hard to understand, the importance of sound method becomes plain. As opposed to Bacon, whose theory implies that the historian must believe everything he is told, Vico recognised the importance of systematic disbelief. But this was not at all the same thing as the superficial "historical Pyrrhonism" fashionable, especially in France, during the seventeenth and eighteenth centuries—the notion that all history is a tissue of legends and fancies, *une fable convenue,* a matter not deserving the attention of enlightened minds. That simple rejection of authority was the mere antithesis of Bacon's simple acceptance, and did little to advance either the practice or the theory of historical research.

Vico went farther than this; probing the depths of scepticism in order to find something deeper than scepticism itself. He looked for the chief sources of historical error, and found them in a tendency to glorify antiquity; a tendency to gratify national conceit; a tendency on the part of historians to think that the people they are studying must have been like themselves—scholars and thinkers; a tendency to think that civilisation must have arisen by "diffusion"; and a tendency to think that early writers must know the facts about early history. The historian must guard against these tendencies by constant appeal to documentary evidence. Narrative is worthless unless founded on, and checked by, documents. Vico shows how etymology, mythology and legend may be used as documents; instead of accepting legend and myth as fact, or rejecting them as fable, he attempts to interpret them as documents revealing the mind and manners of the age that created them.

The importance of Vico lies in the fact that, for him, history becomes an affair neither of accepting nor of rejecting what the "authorities" say, but of interpreting it. The centre of gravity of historical thought is thus placed in the *principles* by which the historian interprets documents. Knowledge does not come flying into the empty mind, as Locke seemed to think, through the windows of the senses; it arises inside the mind when the data of sense are interpreted by principles grounded, as Kant showed, in the nature of the mind itself. So for history; historical knowledge cannot be poured out of one mind into another, it has to be built up by each historian for himself, using the universal and necessary principles of historical thought to interpret the data which the past has left behind it. This fundamental conception is what we owe to Vico.

3. *Universal History: Herder to Hegel*

Lacking a sound conception of its own methods, history can deal with nothing but those periods—mostly quite recent—for which materials are abundant. Towards other, remoter, periods, it can only vacillate between blind acceptance and blind rejection of its authorities. But the discovery of historical method alters all that. It now becomes possible to range a far wider field. Vico's work on the principles of historical criticism rendered futile Voltaire's proposal, half a century later, that historians should confine their attention to the period after the end of the Middle Ages, as the only period concerning which we possessed sound and sufficient information. Gibbon's great history stops where, according to Voltaire, all genuine history begins. Vico's work was not widely known during the eighteenth century, but a number of other men during that century worked on the same lines, and found, like him, that an increasing mastery of historical technique opened up increasingly difficult and obscure fields for research.

The inference was drawn, that it was possible to construct a universal history, a complete history of the world. The world, in the eighteenth century, was not so very old; only about 5,700–5,800 years; and if it was possible to reconstruct inferentially those portions of its history concerning which reliable and explicit authorities were lacking, what was to prevent the historian from rising above all fragmentary and piecemeal narration of this or that partial series of events, and composing a universal history in which every such series should be seen in its proper setting and perspective?

The idea of a universal history was not a new one; but hitherto (in Bossuet, 1627–1704, for instance) it had served rather for edification than as a stimulus to historical research. But now the flood-gates were opened to a new tide of historical literature, all based on the idea that history could be narrated as a whole by the adoption of principles which could serve to correct and to supplement the authorities. From the time of Herder (1744–1803), who used it in the title of a book in 1784, the name "philosophy of history" came to be especially used for this kind of universal history, though that had not been its original sense;

it was apparently invented by Voltaire (1694–1778), and used by him as the name for a new kind of history—what we call social and economic history—which he advocated as more "philosophical" (that is, scientific) than the repetition of old wives' tales about kings and queens. Voltaire did not realise that there might be scientific history about kings and queens, and old wives' tales about social and economic facts.

These "philosophies of history," or universal histories, fell into deserved discredit through their habit of allowing imagination, backed up by pseudo-philosophy, to fill the gaps in historical knowledge. Their common characteristic was that they fitted facts together so as to make a pattern in which the same forms tended to recur again and again. Vico had thought of the Middle Ages as a "return of barbarism," showing the same fundamental features as the barbarism of the Homeric age and all other barbarisms in history; Hegel (1770–1831), not content with so crude a conception, and realising that the difference between Dante and Homer was at least as important as their resemblance, thought of history as a pattern not so much repeating itself as repeating the pattern of logic. The succession of historical periods is at bottom, for Hegel, a logical sequence of concepts, each concept the keynote of a period. Any idea of this kind is open to the fatal objection that it encourages the historian to plug the holes in his knowledge with something that is not history, because it has not been extracted from his sources. This objection points to a fundamental flaw in the very idea of a universal history—the fact that it claims a kind of universality which by its nature history can never possess. All history is the history of something, something definite and particular; the history of everything is the history of nothing. This tells equally against belated specimens of the same type of thought; the historical materialism of Marx (1818–1883), with its pattern of economic historical phases; Comte's (1798–1857) law of the "three stages," theological, metaphysical, and positive, through which all ideas must pass;

Spencer's (1820–1903) evolution from the uniform and homogeneous to the diversified and heterogeneous; or, to come down to the present day, Spengler's succession of "cultures" all rigidly moulded on the same abstract pattern.

So obvious to us is the futility of these universal histories, that we can afford to consider their merits; for they had great merits in their time, which was the late eighteenth and early nineteenth centuries. First, they showed that people realised the importance of principles and methods, and had got rid of the Baconian idea that history was a mere exercise of memory. If Buckle was justified when he said in 1857 that "any author who from indolence of thought, or from natural incapacity, is unfit to deal with the highest branches of knowledge, has only to pass some years in reading a certain number of books, and then he is qualified to be an historian," the historians of whom he spoke had learnt nothing from Vico, Herder, or Hegel. Secondly, they showed that people were trying to solve the difficult problems, instead of being content (as Voltaire would have had them be) with the easy ones. They were guilty, no doubt, of culpable rashness in this attempt, but the attempt itself was a step in advance. And thirdly, their results, however unsatisfactory, stimulated further historical research by summing up, as it were, the present state of knowledge, and thereby calling attention to its defects. The nineteenth century saw an unparalleled development of historical technique and historical knowledge; and this is closely connected with the fact that it began with this gallant but unsuccessful attempt at universal "philosophical" history.

4. The Distinction between History and Science: Schopenhauer to Windelband

At bottom, the attempt to construct a universal history failed because it involved a confusion between history and science. They are both forms of knowledge, involving observation and thought, and requiring highly-developed technical methods; thus they have much in common, and a good deal of light can be thrown on history by calling attention to the resemblance between it and science. But there is also a difference. In science, the individual fact is of importance only so far as it illustrates a general law. The law is the end, the fact is the means to it. Whether Newton's apple really fell or not, hardly matters so long as we grasp Newton's law of gravitation. In history, the opposite is true. The individual fact is the end, and the general law is of importance only so far as it enables us to determine the fact. Whether bad money invariably drives out good, is a question not for the historian, but for the economist, who is a kind of scientist; but the historian may appeal to this principle as an aid in discovering what happened on a certain occasion.

Now, the mistake of the universal histories was that they did not take facts seriously enough. They did not realise that every fact is unique and not to be replaced by any other. When they plugged a hole in their knowledge by inventing a fact, what they invented was not an individual but simply any instance of some general law. The astronomers who invented Neptune in order to account for the irregularities in the orbit of Uranus were quite right, but only because they were astronomers. The hypothetical Neptune, to them, was *any* planet of the required mass and in the required place. That is how an astronomer ought to think of a planet. But to think of Augustus as *any* man who fulfills the condition of founding the Roman Principate is absurd. Yet that is how historical facts are actually thought of by this kind of history. The historians had allowed science to go to their heads.

To get away from this false theory, with its disastrous practical consequences, it was necessary to emphasize the distinction between the individuality of the historian's object and the generality of the scientist's. This was the contribution which the nineteenth century made to the philosophy of history.

Early in the century, Schopenhauer (1788–1860) had already called attention to this truth. He stated with perfect clearness that the business of history is to determine individual facts, the business of science to determine general laws. So far, he was only saying what had been a commonplace ever since Aristotle; the same thing had been repeatedly said, for instance, by Leibniz (1646–1716) and his followers, in the seventeenth and eighteenth centuries. But previously the moral had always been "so much the worse for history." Genuine knowledge, it had been currently believed since at least Plato's time, must be universal, not particular; necessary, not contingent; of eternal truths, not of transitory facts. Indeed, it was in the course of an attempt to rescue history from this reproach that the universal histories had been constructed. But Schopenhauer, though he drew the same moral and poured scorn on history as a form of knowledge which "crawls about on the common earth of experience" instead of "rising above it into the air of thought," went on, quite inconsistently, to maintain that history has a unique and very necessary function: namely to give a people a knowledge of its own past and thus lead it to understand itself. These two inconsistent attitudes towards history are drawn, the one from seventeenth-century rationalism, the other from the romantic movement, with its profound sense of history as revealing the roots of national character.

The conviction that the individuality of history, its insistence on the individual fact instead of the general law, was not a defect of history, but just its essence, gathered weight as the century went on. It was reinforced, first, by the increasing discredit of the so-called "philosophies of history," and, secondly, by the utter bankruptcy of attempts, like that of Buckle, to "raise history to the rank of a science" by extracting general laws from it. Historians, as they came to know their own business better, confessed their disgust for these things, and found that the only people who indulged in them were people who knew very little history and had very little desire to learn more. They discovered, for instance, that Comte's "sociology," instead of being an improved history, was only "history in which it didn't matter whether the facts were right or wrong," in other words, it was science and not history at all.

By the end of the nineteenth century, people who were studying the philosophy of history in a competent and serious way had everywhere come to an agreement that history was knowledge of the individual, and this conviction had in most cases enabled them to reject the old philosophies of history, and the later attempts to confuse history with science, but it had done no more. "A *science* of the *individual*," Schopenhauer had said, "is a contradiction in terms." Try as they might, the nineteenth-century thinkers could not get round that. Some, like Lazarus and Steinthal (collaborating about 1860), tried to explain history as "intuitive" knowledge; but that destroyed its reasoned, scientific, inferential character. Others, like Windelband in an address of 1894, tried to divide concepts into two kinds, in such a way as to make room for this logical monstrosity, a science of the individual, within the theory of knowledge. The history of German thought on the subject in the later nineteenth century—outside Germany the problem was generally ignored—is the history of a series of attempts, uniformly unsuccessful, to meet Schopenhauer's challenge and explain how historical thought could be *wissenschaftlich* and yet have individual facts for its object. The positive value of these failures lies in the fact that they did state the real question at issue, and thereby showed that historians were gaining courage to resist the tyranny of natural science.

5. The Individual or Historical Judgment: Croce

Only one really fertile suggestion was made during this period, and this was made by a young Italian, whose experience of historical work and literary criticism gave him a fresh and first-hand view of the subject. Having realised that the business of the artist is to "see" individual men, landscapes, tunes, and so forth ("intuition"), and that the business of the historian is to "see" individual historical events, Benedetto Croce, in 1893, boldly drew the conclusion that art and history were the same thing. This pronouncement had nothing to do with the trite observation that the historian must be also an artist in so far as he must, incidentally, express himself in prose which ought, therefore, to be good prose. Clio, for Croce, was not merely a muse; she was identical with Polyhymnia.

This did not solve the problem, but it brought matters to a head. It revealed the bankruptcy of German thought that no one in that country was able to reply effectively to Croce. The initiative lay with him, and he disposed of his critics with perfect ease (Croce, *Primi Saggi,* 1919, reprints the original essay on *History subsumed under the General Concept of Art* and selections from the controversy that followed it). The subsequent development of his thought (in *Logica,* 1909, and *Teoria e Storia della Storiografia,* 1913—the latter by far the most important work of our time on the subject) does not so much retract the original statement as modify the general theory of knowledge in such a way as to remove its paradoxical appearance.

The essence of this development is the doctrine of the individual judgment. Ordinary logic distinguishes the individual judgment, "This *S* is *P*," from the the universal judgment "All *S* is *P*." Now, says Croce, "This *S* is *P*" is history, "All *S* is *P*" is science. But whenever we say "All *S* is *P*" we have before our minds a "this *S*." When we try to think out the universal nature of gravitation or justice or poetry, we do it by inquiring into *this* gravitating body, *this* just act, *this* poem, and finding in them the expression of the necessary nature of gravitation, justice, or poetry in general. "All *S* is *P*" means "This *S*, in its character as *S*, is *P*." When the element of individuality is taken away, we have, not a universal judgment "All *S* is *P*," but nothing at all.

This conception can be expressed by saying that all knowledge is historical knowledge (individual judgment) and that science is history with its individual reference neglected. There is nothing in science that there is not in history, except this neglect. The rationality of science lies not in the form "All *S* is *P*" but in the predicate *P,* which is a concept, a universal idea properly thought out. When I say "Alexander VI was unscrupulous," there is a whole system of moral philosophy contained in the word unscrupulous, and in plain terms this means that I have no business to say it unless I am able to explain what I mean by unscrupulous, and explain it satisfactorily. The individual judgment of history contains within itself, in the shape of its own predicate, the universality of science; and history is shown to be, not something that falls short of scientific accuracy and rationality and demonstrativeness, but something that possesses all this and, going beyond it, finds it exemplified in an individual fact.

III. OUTLINE OF A PHILOSOPHY OF HISTORY

History is knowledge of the past, and the past consists of events that have finished happening. The past does not exist and cannot be perceived; our knowledge of it is not derived from observation, and cannot be verified by experiment. "A realistic" theory, according to which knowledge is the "apprehension of a really existing object," is ruled out as absolutely inapplicable to history.

We come to know the past, not immediately, but by interpreting evidence. This evidence (or data) is something that exists in the present and is perceived by the historian. How he comes to perceive it, we are not here asking.

But data are not enough. They must be interpreted. This requires principles, and the body of principles constitutes historical method or technique. Some of these principles are scientific in character, that is, they concern particular groups of evidence, and compose the special sciences of archaeology, palaeography, numismatics, and so forth. Some are philosophical, that is, they apply universally to all evidence whatever, and compose the logic of historical method. It is to this that we must refer such problems as, the nature and limits of negative evidence, the possibility of analogical argument, and so forth.

Data, on the one hand, and principles of interpretation, on the other, are the two elements of all historical thought. But they do not exist separately and then undergo a combination. They exist together or not at all. The historian cannot first collect data and then interpret them. It is only when he has a problem in his mind that he can begin to search for data bearing on it. Anything whatever may serve him as data, if he can find out how to interpret it. The historian's data are the entire present.

The beginning of historical research is therefore not the collection or contemplation of crude facts as yet uninterpreted, but the asking of a question which sets one off looking for facts which may help one to answer it. All historical research is focussed in this way upon some particular question or problem which defines its subject. And the question must be asked with some reasonable expectation of being able to answer it, and to answer it by genuinely historical thinking; otherwise it leads nowhere, it is at best idle "wondering," not the focus of a piece of historical work. We express this by saying that a question does or does not "arise." To say that a question arises, is to say that it has a logical connexion with our previous thoughts, that we have a reason for asking it and are not moved by mere capricious curiosity.

This conception of history clears up the difficulties—insoluble on any other theory—that surround the ideas of selection, specialisation, "periodising" and so forth. For practical purposes, experience shows that historians must divide history into "periods," must "specialise," must "select." But if the past is a solid mass of existing fact waiting to be "apprehended" by the historian, these things cannot be done except in an arbitrary and capricious way, a way which makes it impossible to dignify historical thought with the name of knowledge. The solution of this problem is that the historian does not select, because no past facts are "there" before him, to select from, until he has put them there by sheer historical thinking. His selection or specialisation consists merely in dealing with the questions that arise in the course of his study. He does not neglect the others; not having arisen, they are not there to be neglected.

Since past facts do not exist, there is no such thing as a total body of past facts which a sufficiently accomplished historian might know in its totality and, if he had time, write out in a universal history. The attempt at a universal history is foredoomed to failure. All history must be the history of something particular, and the most we can ever do is to express the present state of knowledge concerning this particular subject. As no history can be universal, so no history can be final. Yet every history can be universal in the sense that it can really cover the ground it professes to cover, and can be final in the sense that it can really state where our knowledge of its subject stands at the present time.

All history is thus an interim report on the progress made in the study of its subject down to the present; and hence all history is at the same time the history of history, for example, any monograph on the battle of Marathon must summarise, explicitly or implicitly, the entire history of research concerning the battle of Marathon. For the same reason, all history brings its narrative down to the present day; not necessarily as history, but as the history of history. This is why every age must write history afresh. Everyone brings his own mind to the study of history, and approaches it from the point of view which is characteristic of himself and his generation; naturally, therefore, one age, one man, sees in a particular historical event things which another does not, and *vice versa*. The attempt to eliminate this "subjective element" from history is always insincere—it means keeping your own point of view while asking other people to give up theirs—and always unsuccessful. If it succeeded, history itself would vanish. This does not reduce history to something arbitrary or capricious. It remains genuine knowledge. How can this be, if my thoughts about Julius Caesar differ from Mommsen's? Must not one of us be wrong? No, because the object differs. My historical thought is about my own past, not about Mommsen's past. Mommsen and I share in a great many things, and in many respects we share in a common past; but in so far as we are different people and representatives of different cultures and different generations we have behind us different pasts, and everything in his past has to undergo a slight alteration before it can enter into mine. Quite apart, then, from any error in his or my interpretation of the evidence, our views of Julius Caesar must differ, slightly perhaps, but perceptibly. This difference is not arbitrary, for I can see—or ought to be able to see—that in his place, apart (once more) from all question of error, I should have come to his conclusions.

Finally, since the past in itself is nothing, the knowledge of the past in itself is not, and cannot be, the historian's goal. His goal, as the goal of a thinking being, is knowledge of the present; to that everything must return, round that everything must revolve. But, as historian, he is concerned with one special aspect of the present—how it came to be what it is. In that sense, the past is an aspect or function of the present; and that is how it must always appear to the historian who reflects intelligently on his own work, or, in other words, attempts a philosophy of history.

BIBLIOGRAPHY

A. COLLINGWOOD'S PHILOSOPHICAL WRITINGS

"Aesthetic," *The Mind*. Edited by R. J. S. McDowall. London: Longmans, Green and Co., 1927.

"Are History and Science Different Kinds of Knowledge?" *Mind*, XXXI (1922), 443–451.

"Art," *Oxford History of England*. Edited by G. N. Clark. Oxford: Clarendon Press, 1936.

Autobiography, An. London: Oxford University Press, 1939.

"Can the New Idealism Dispense with Mysticism?" *Proceedings of the Aristotelian Society*, Supplement, III (1923), 161–175.

"Croce's Philosophy of History," *Hibbert Journal*, XIX (1921), 263–278.

"Devil, The," *Concerning Prayer*. Edited by B. H. Streeter and others. London: Macmillan Co., 1916.

"Economics as a Philosophical Science," *International Journal of Ethics*, XXXVI (1926), 162–185.

Essay on Metaphysics, An. Oxford: Clarendon Press, 1940.

Essay on Philosophical Method, An. Oxford: Clarendon Press, 1933.

Faith and Reason. London: Ernest Benn, 1928.

"Fascism and Nazism," *Philosophy*, XV (1940), 168–176.

First Mate's Log of a Voyage to Greece in the Schooner Yacht FLEUR DE LYS in 1939, The. London: Oxford University Press, 1940.

"Form and Content in Art," *Journal of Philosophical Studies*, IV (1929), 332–345.

Historical Imagination, The. Oxford: Clarendon Press, 1935.

Human Nature and Human History. London: H. Milford, 1936.

"Human Nature and Human History," *Proceedings of the British Academy,* XXII (1937), 97–127.

Idea of History, The. Oxford: Clarendon Press, 1946.

Idea of Nature, The. Oxford: Clarendon Press, 1945.

"Limits of Historical Knowledge, The," *Journal of Philosophical Studies,* III (1928), 213–222.

"Nature and Aims of a Philosophy of History, The," *Proceedings of the Aristotelian Society,* XXV (1924–1925), 151–174.

New Leviathan, The. Oxford: Clarendon Press, 1942.

"On the So-called Idea of Causation," *Proceedings of the Aristotelian Society,* XXXVIII (1937–1938), 85–112.

"Oswald Spengler and the Theory of Historical Cycles," *Antiquity,* I (1927), 311–325.

Outlines of a Philosophy of Art. London: Oxford University Press, 1925.

Philosophy of History, The. London: G. Bell and Sons, Ltd., 1930.

"Philosophy of Progress, A," *The Realist,* I (1929), 64–77.

"Place of Art in Education, The," *Hibbert Journal,* XXIV (1926), 434–448.

"Plato's Philosophy of Art," *Mind,* XXXIV (1925), 154–172.

"Political Action," *Proceedings of the Aristotelian Society,* XXIX (1928–1929), 155–176.

Principles of Art, The. Oxford: Clarendon Press, 1938.

"Reason is Faith Cultivating Itself," *Hibbert Journal,* XXVI (1927), 3–14.

Religion and Philosophy. London: Macmillan and Co., Ltd., 1916.

"Religion, Science, and Philosophy," *Truth and Freedom,* II (1926).

Ruskin's Philosophy. Kendal: T. Wilson and Son, 1920.

"Sensation and Thought," *Proceedings of the Aristotelian Society,* XXIV (1923–1924), 55–76.

"Some Perplexities about Time: with an Attempted Solution," *Proceedings of the Aristotelian Society,* XXVI (1925–1926), 135–150.

Speculum Mentis. Oxford: Clarendon Press, 1924.

"Theory of Historical Cycles, The," *Antiquity,* I (1927), 435–446.

Three Laws of Politics, The. London: Oxford University Press, 1941.

"What is the Problem of Evil?" *Theology,* I (1920).

B. COLLINGWOOD'S HISTORICAL AND ARCHAEOLOGICAL WRITINGS[1]

Archaeology of Roman Britain, The. London: Methuen and Co., Ltd., 1930.

Roman Britain. Revised. Oxford: Clarendon Press, 1934.

Roman Britain and the English Settlements. 2nd. edition. With J. M. L. Myers. Oxford: Clarendon Press, 1936.

C. COLLINGWOOD'S TRANSLATIONS

Croce, B. "Aesthetic," *Encyclopedia Britannica,* 14th edition, 1929.
————. *An Autobiography.* Oxford: Clarendon Press, 1927.
————. *The Philosophy of Giambattista Vico.* London: Allen and Unwin, 1913.
de Ruggiero, G. *The History of European Liberalism.* London: Oxford University Press, 1927.
————. *Modern Philosophy.* London: Allen and Unwin, 1921.

D. LITERATURE ON COLLINGWOOD

Buchdahl, Gerd. "Has Collingwood Been Unfortunate in His Critics?" *Australasian Journal of Philosophy,* XXXVI (1958), 95–108.
Bultmann, Rudolph. *History and Eschatology.* Edinburgh: Edinburgh University Press, 1957.
Casserley, J. V. L. *The Christian in Philosophy.* London: Faber and Faber, 1949.
Cohen, L. Jonathan. "Has Collingwood Been Misinterpreted?" *Philosophical Quarterly,* VII (1957), 149–150.
————. "A Survey of Work in the Philosophy of History," *Philosophical Quarterly,* II (1952), 172–186.
Donagan, Alan. "The Croce-Collingwood Theory of Art," *Philosophy,* XXXIII (1958), 162–167.

---

[1] Only Collingwood's books have been listed. A bibliography of over 150 pamphlets, articles, and reviews can be found in *Proceedings of the British Academy,* XXIX (1944), 481–485.

————. *The Later Philosophy of R. G. Collingwood*. Oxford: Clarendon Press, 1962.

————. "The Verification of Historical Theses," *Philosophical Quarterly*, VI (1956), 193–208.

Dray, William. *Laws and Explanation in History*. London: Oxford University Press, 1957.

————. "R. G. Collingwood and the Acquaintance Theory of Knowledge," *Revue internationale de philosophie*, XI (1957), 420–432.

————. "R. G. Collingwood on Reflective Thought," *Journal of Philosophy*, LVII (1960), 153–163.

Ducasse, C. J. "Mr. Collingwood on Philosophical Method," *Journal of Philosophy*, XXXIII (1936), 95–106.

Flenley, R. "Collingwood's Idea of History," *Canadian Historical Review*, XXVII (1947), 68–72.

Fruchon, P. "Signification de l'histoire de la philosophie selon l'autobiographie de Collingwood," *Les Etudes philosophiques*, XIII (1958), 143–160.

Gardiner, P. *The Nature of Historical Explanation*. London: Oxford University Press, 1952.

————. "The 'Objects' of Historical Knowledge," *Philosophy*, XXVII (1952), 211–220.

Grant, G. K. "Collingwood's Theory of Historical Knowledge," *Renaissance and Modern Studies*, I (1957), 65–90.

Harris, Errol E. "Collingwood on Eternal Problems," *Philosophical Quarterly*, I (1951), 228–241.

————. "Collingwood's Theory of History," *Philosophical Quarterly*, VII (1957), 35–49.

————. "Mr. Collingwood and the Ontological Argument; Reply to G. Ryle," *Mind*, XLV (1936), 474–480.

————. *Nature, Mind and Modern Science*. London: George Allen and Unwin Ltd., 1954.

————. "Objectivity and Reason," *Philosophy*, XXXI (1956), 55–73.

Harris, R. W. "Collingwood's *Idea of History*," *History*, XXXVII (1952), 1–7.

Hartt, J. N. "Metaphysics, History, and Civilization: Collingwood's

Account of Their Interrelationships," *Journal of Religion*, XXXIII (1953), 198–211.

Hearnshaw, L. S. "A Reply to Collingwood's Attack on Psychology," *Mind*, LI (1942), 160–169.

Hodges, Herbert A. *Philosophy of Wilhelm Dilthey*. London: Routledge and Kegan Paul, Ltd., 1952.

Hospers, John. "The Croce-Collingwood Theory of Art," *Philosophy*, XXXI (1956), 291–308.

Knox, T. M. "Notes on Collingwood's Philosophical Work," *Proceedings of the British Academy*, XXIX (1944), 469–475.

Langer, Susanne K. *Feeling and Form*. New York: Charles Scribner's Sons, 1953.

Lewelyn, J. L. "Collingwood's Doctrine of Absolute Presuppositions," *Philosophical Quarterly*, II (1961), 49–60.

Mackay, Donald S. "On Supposing and Presupposing," *Review of Metaphysics*, II (1948), 1–20.

McCallum, R. B. "Robin George Collingwood," *Proceedings of the British Academy*, XXIX (1944), 463–468.

Molina, Fernando R. "Collingwood on Philosophical Methodology," *Ideas*, VI (1957), 1–14.

Mure, G. R. G. "Benedetto Croce and Oxford," *Philosophical Quarterly*, IV (1954), 327–331.

Myers, E. D. "A Note on Collingwood's Criticism of Toynbee," *Journal of Philosophy*, XLIV (1947), 485–489.

Pardinas Illanes, Felipe. "Dilthey y Collingwood," *Filosofía y letras*, XIX (1950), 87–105.

Richmond, I. A. "Appreciation of R. G. Collingwood as an Archaeologist," *Proceedings of the British Academy*, XXIX (1944), 476–480.

Ritchie, A. D. "The Logic of Question and Answer," *Mind*, LII (1943), 24–38.

Rotenstreich, N. "From Facts to Thoughts, Collingwood's Views on the Nature of History," *Philosophy*, XXXV (1960), 122–137.

———. "Historicism and Philosophy: Reflections on R. G. Collingwood," *Revue internationale de philosophie*, XI (1957), 401–419.

Ryle, Gilbert. "Back to the Ontological Argument; Rejoinder," *Mind*, XLV (1937), 53–57.

————. "Mr. Collingwood and the Ontological Argument," *Mind*, XLIV (1935), 137–151.

————. *Philosophical Arguments.* Oxford: Clarendon Press, 1946.

Schneider, Frederick D. "Collingwood and the Idea of History," *University of Toronto Quarterly*, XXII (1952–1953), 172–183.

Shalom, Albert. "R. G. Collingwood *et la metaphysique*," *Les Etudes philosophiques*, X (1955), 693–711.

Strauss, Leo. "On Collingwood's Philosophy of History," *Review of Metaphysics*, V (1952), 559–586.

Tomlin, E. W. F. *R. G. Collingwood.* London: Longmans, Green and Co., 1953.

Toynbee, Arnold J. *A Study of History.* 12 Vols. London: Oxford University Press, 1934–1961. See IX (1954), 718–737.

Voegelin, Eric. "The Oxford Political Philosophers," *Philosophical Quarterly*, III (1943), 97–114.

Walpole, H. "R. G. Collingwood and the Idea of Language," *University of Wichita Bulletin*, XXXVIII (1963), 3–8.

Walsh, W. H. *An Introduction to Philosophy of History.* London: Hutchinson and Co., Ltd., 1951.

————. *Reason and Experience.* Oxford: Clarendon Press, 1947.

————. "R. G. Collingwood's Philosophy of History," *Philosophy*, XXII (1947), 153–160.

White, Hayden V. "Collingwood and Toynbee: Transitions in English Historical Thought," *English Miscellany*, VIII (1957), 147–178.

E. REVIEWS OF COLLINGWOOD'S PHILOSOPHICAL BOOKS

Autobiography, An. Reviewed in: *Journal of Philosophical Studies*, XV (1940), 88–90; *Journal of Philosophy*, XXXVI (1939), 717; *Manchester Guardian*, August 15, 1939, p. 5; *New Statesman*, XVIII (1939), 222; *Spectator*, CLXIII (1939), 262; *Times* (London) *Literary Supplement*, August 5, 1939, p. 464.

Essay on Metaphysics, An. Reviewed in: *Journal of Philosophical Studies*, XVI (1941), 74–78; *Journal of Philosophy*, XXXVIII (1941), 48; *Manchester Guardian*, May 6, 1940, p. 7; *Mind*, L (1941), 184–190; *Nature*, CXLVIII (1941), 7; *New York Times*,

December, 1940, p. 47; *Times* (London) *Literary Supplement,* May 18, 1940, p. 240.

Essay on Philosophical Method, An. Reviewed in: *American Review,* IV (1935), 627; *International Journal of Ethics,* XLIV (1934), 357; *Journal of Philosophical Studies,* IX (1934), 350–352; *Nature,* CXXXIV (1934), 648; *Times* (London) *Literary Supplement,* March 1, 1934, p. 136.

Human Nature and Human History. Reviewed in: *Journal of Philosophical Studies,* XII (1937), 233–236.

Idea of History, The. Reviewed in: *Australasian Journal of Philosophy,* XXVI (1948), 94–114; *Book Week,* December 1, 1946, p. 12; *Canadian Historical Review,* XXVIII (1947), 68–72; *Hibbert Journal,* XLV (1946), 83–86; *Historische Zeitschrift,* CLXXXIV (1957), 594–597; *History,* XXXVII (1952), 1–7; *Journal of Philosophy,* XLIV (1947), 184–188; *Journal of Religion,* XXXIII (1953), 198–211; *Manchester Guardian,* August 7, 1946, p. 3; *Philosophical Review,* LVI (1947), 587–592; *Philosophy,* XXII (1947), 153–160; *Philosophy,* XXVII (1952), 211–220; *Review of Metaphysics,* V (1952), 559–586; *Spectator,* CLXXVII (1946), 172; *Times* (London) *Literary Supplement,* August 17, 1946, p. 385; *University of Toronto Quarterly,* XXII (1952–1953), 172–183.

Idea of Nature, The. Reviewed in: *Journal of Philosophical Studies,* XX (1945), 260–261; *Philosophical Review,* LV (1946), 199–202.

New Leviathan, The. Reviewed in: *American Political Science Review,* XXXVII (1943), 724; *Annals of the American Academy,* CCXXIX (1943), 181; *Foreign Affairs,* XXII (1943), 155; *Journal of Philosophical Studies,* XVIII (1943), 75–80; *New York Times,* August 1, 1943, p. 16; *Political Science Quarterly,* LVIII (1943), 435.

Outlines of a Philosophy of Art. Reviewed in: *Boston Transcript,* August 1, 1925, p. 2; *Nature,* CXVI (1925), 116; *Times* (London) *Literary Supplement,* April 16, 1925, p. 269.

Principles of Art, The. Reviewed in: *Journal of Philosophical Studies,* XIII (1938), 492–496; *Manchester Guardian,* May 27, 1938, p. 7;

Nation, CXLVIII (1939), 98; *New Republic*, XCVII (1939), 296; *New York Times*, July 17, 1938, p. 4; *Times* (London) *Literary Supplement*, August 13, 1938, p. 533.

Speculum Mentis. Reviewed in: *Catholic World*, CXXII (1925), 128; *International Journal of Ethics*, XXXV (1925), 323; *Literary Review*, May, 1925, p. 5.

INDEX

Achilles: 100
actions, human: explaining of, xxii–xxiii; as expression of thoughts, xxvi–xxviii
Admiralty Intelligence Division: x
Alcibiades: 126
Alexander, Hartley Burr: x
Alexander the Great: relation of, to Caesar, 59–60; mentioned, 47
Alexandria, Egypt: 93
America: philosophy of history in, ix
Amos (prophet): 125–126
annals: relation of, to history, 6, 8, 9, 10; as willed, 7; thought in, 7
Anthropology: 25
Arabia, culture of: Christ in, 60; monotheism of, 62
archaeology: 31, 136
architecture: and cultural differences, 60; value judgment in, 78–80, 82–83; Norman and Gothic, 109–111; history of, 112; progress in, 116–118
Aristotle: on history-science relation, 23–24, 23 n. 2, 25, 133; and progress, 107; philosophy of history of, 126; mentioned, xxix, 3
Arnold, Matthew: 107–108
art: object of, 45; relation of, to history, 45, 48, 49, 135; and cultural differences, 60; value judgments in, 78–84 *passim*, 109–111; philosophy of, 122; and function of artist, 134

Aston Villa: 124
Athene: 62
Athens: people of, 82; constitution of, 90; mentioned, 84
Augustus Octavian: 116, 132
authority. SEE sources, historical
Autobiography, An: xi, xxxi, xxxii

Bach, Johann Sebastian: 83
Bacon, Francis: philosophy of history of, 126, 127; mentioned, xxxiii, 131
Baroque period: 74, 82–83
Becket, Saint Thomas à: 78
Bede, the Venerable: 80
Beelzebub: 64
Bellicia: 79, 80, 81
Bergson, Henri: school of, 25
Berkeley, George: on universal-particular relation, 24, 25–26
Bernini, Giovanni Lorenzo: 83
Bewcastle cross: 80, 83
Birkenhead, Lord: 93
Black Death, the: 84
Bonaparte, Napoleon. *See* Napoleon I
Bosanquet, Bernard: 90, 95
Bossuet, Jaques: 129
Bramble, Matthew: 78 n.
British Academy: x
Brutus: xxvii
Buckle, Henry Thomas: on historians, 131; on history as science, 133

cay of, 69–70, 73–74; SEE ALSO
Greece, ancient; Rome, ancient
—,Magian: monotheism of, 62, 64;
rise of, 66, 69–70, 73–74
cultures: morphology of historical,
60–61, 67; unity of plurality of,
71; origin and development of,
72; SEE ALSO *Decline of the
West;* history, cyclical theories
of
cyclical history. SEE history,
theories of (cyclical)

Dante Alighieri: 130
Dark Ages: knowledge of, 88–89
decadence, theory of: and dark
ages, 80–81; rejection of, 81–84;
simplicity of, 106; validity of,
106; and optimism in opposition,
106–108; as matter of temperament, 108–109. SEE ALSO progress
Decline of the West: Spengler's
historical sense in, xxxiv, 61–62,
67–68, 71, 72; proving cultural
differences in, 60
—, cyclical theory of: basic statement of, 57; phases of culture
in, 57–59, 72, 131; parallel fig-
ures in, 58–60; homology in, 59–
60; originality of, 60–61; and
dominant characteristic of culture, 63–65, 71–72; cultural re-
lationships in, 65–66, 69–70, 71,
72; and predetermination of
future, xxxiv, 68–70, 71; and
determining past, 68–69, 70–71;
compared to Vico's and Hegel's,
72
de Ruggiero, G.: 22
Descartes, Rene: interpretation of,
61; on historical veracity, 91;
and philosophy of science, 127
drama, Aristophanic: 64

dualism: of history and annals, 6–
10 *passim;* realness of, 8–9; of
error and truth, 12; of thought
and life, 13–14, 15; of theoretical and practical man, 14; of
idea and fact, 21. SEE ALSO
knowledge, history and science
as

Eclogue (Virgil): 107
Economics: 25
education: English, classics in, 4;
Italian, and Croce, 21; classical,
4, 65–66
Edwardes, Kathleen Frances: xi
Egypt, culture of: phase of, 58;
parallel figure in, 69; architecture of, 117
empiricism: 25
England: philosophy of history in,
ix; education in, 4; mentioned,
93
Epicureans: 61
Epicurus: worlds of, 66
Erigena: 80
error: nature of, 11–12; and
Croce's naturalist-idealist conflict, 11–13 *passim;* as act of
will, 12; philosophical, origin of,
12–13; historical, source of, 128
Essay on Metaphysics, The: xi
*Essay on Philosophical Method,
An:* xi
Euclid: geometry of, 65, 71, 95
evidence, historical: and history as
science, xiv–xv, xxxiii; and criterion for authority, xiv–xv; and
interpolation, xviii–xix, xx, xxii,
52; and other evidence, xxi, xxii,
94; and historical events, xxvii;
relation of, to historical problem, 53; nature of, 92; limitations of, 92–94; reliance on, 94,
95; in historical thinking, 99,

happened, xvi, xxii–xxix, xvi; and interpolation, xviii–xx, xxi, xxii, xxvii, xxix, Collingwood on nature of, xix, xxi–xxii; evidence of, xix–xx, 92; as revisable and incomplete, xx–xxi; compared to other knowledge, xx–xxii, 95; and realist theory of knowledge, xxxiii; intersubjective character of, xxxiv; and cyclical theory, 88, 89; as transitory, 90; as doubtful, 90–91, 94–95; and historical thought and scepticism, 91, 100; limits of, 100–101; and past-present relationship, 101–102; and historical method, 124–125; and principles for interpretation, 128; development of, and universal histories, 131; as individual judgment, 135–136; universality of science in, 136. SEE ALSO evidence, historical; history; scepticism, historical; sources, historical

—, methods of: and criticism of sources, 51–52; and historical knowledge, 124–125; and principles for interpretation, 127–128, 136–137; and range of study, 129; and universal histories, 131

—, studies in: Collingwood's defense of, xxxiii; range of, 54, 129; flourishing of, period of, 91; and skepticism, 91; necessary assumption in, 95; inspection of, 95–96, 103 and n.; correct answer in, 97–98; scientific value of, 103; and idea of progress, 111; and universal history, 129, 131; historical problem in, 137–138.

— and historical thought: generalization and inductive thinking

in, 35–36; attitude of, toward facts, 44, 46–47, 49; study of, as philosophy of history, 44, 45; as concrete, 45, 46; historians' concern with, 47, 48, 67; and perception, 49, 50; and historical problems, 52–53; monadic nature of, 55; and historical skepticism, 91, 99–100; and interpretive error, 91–92; definition of, 98–99, 102; principles of, in historical method, 128. SEE ALSO Germany, thought of

history: as philosophy of history, xii; and foretelling future, xii, 68, 112–113; problems of, xvi, 54–55; value of, xvi, xxix–xxxi, 133; as study of human activity, xxiii; distinction of, from psychology, xxix–xxx; relation of, to annals, 5–10 passim; as thought, 7, 18–19; subjectivity in, 11, 54, 138–139; positivity of, 13–16; controversy in, 14–15; compared to poetry, 23–24; cognition as, 25–26; and past, 32, 85, 91, 100–101, 124, 136; critical thought in, 32, 45; generalization in, 35, 40; object of, 45, 46, 99; and art, 45, 48, 49, 135; and historical judgments, 46 and n., 53; objectivity of, 46–47, 55, 56; and historians' self-knowledge, 47; and the history of history, 47, 138; as perception, 49, 50; conclusions of, and sources, 53; as finite thinking, 56; treatment of likenesses in, 59–60; distinction of, from nature, 67–68, 112–113; and understanding other cultures, 70–71; as development, 73, 74–75, 87, 111; judgment of, 76; decadence in, 80, 81–84; past-present relation in, 86, 139; unity and plurality of, 85–86; interpretation of, 87–88; as doubtful, 102–103; and question of progress, 113; as trade or profession, 123; as universal, 123, 124, 130, 138; and philosophy of history development, 125; and the particular, 130; law-fact relation in, 132, 133; function of, 133; method of knowing, 136; as final, 138. SEE ALSO historian; historiography; history, philosophy of; individual, the, and history; knowledge, history and science as; philosophy, relation of, to history; progress; science, and history; universal history

—, events of: *in toto*, and philosophy of history, xii; "inside-outside" theory of, xvi–xvii, xxiv; as expression of thoughts, xxvii–xxviii; as right, 13, 14; relation between, 36–37, 39

—, facts of: relation between, xxxiii; and generalization, 35, 36, 41; as ascertained, 41–43; as an historical question, 42; historians' knowledge of, 43, 53, 55; in historical thought, 44, 46–47, 56; nature of, 47, 52, 132

—, judgment of. SEE decadence, theory of; progress

—, periods of: coherence of, 37; fabrication of, 74, 137–138; characteristics of, 88. SEE ALSO cultures

—, plot (plan) of: conceptions of, 36–37, 38–40; and philosophy of history, 36, 38, 39–40; argument for, 37–38; proper use of, 40–41; and idea of progress, 111–112

—, theories of. SEE Bacon, Francis;

Collingwood, Robin George; Croce, Benedetto: decadence, theory of; history, theories of (cyclical); progress; universal history

—, theories of (cyclical): history of, 57; of Hegel, 57, 72; of Vico, 57, 60, 72; morphology of cultures as, 60–61; and ideas within culture, 72, 73, 74; and relationship between cultures, 72, 73–74; and usefulness of periods, 74; possibility of constructing, 75; and point of view, 75, 88, 105 n.; decadent ages in, 82; and historical knowledge, 89; necessity of, 89; agreement among, 89; and theory of progress, 105 and n.; objection to, 105–106. SEE ALSO *Decline of the West*

history, philosophy of: definition of, ix; as defining history, xii, xv, 126; and prediction, xii, xxxiii–xxxiv; as discovery of general laws, xii, xxxiii, 34, 35–36, 40–41; and history as science, xv, xxxiii; and meaning of history, xxxiii; and plan of history, 34, 38, 39–41, 125; and ascertained facts, 42; as study of historical thinking, 44–45; and the universal, 122, 123, 124; and history as trade, 123–124; function of, 124; and pre-seventeenth-century ideas of history, 125–126; and historical knowledge, 126, 139; modern, 127; universal history as, 129; as social and economic history, 130; 19th century contribution to, 132. SEE ALSO Collingwood, Robin George

History, Philosophy of: 25

history, "scissors-and-paste." SEE "scissors-and-paste" history

156 ESSAYS IN THE PHILOSOPHY OF HISTORY

Logica: 12, 135
London, England: x
Lorenzo, tomb of: 82
Ludovisi throne: 80
Luther, Martin: xxvi

Mach, Ernst: school of, 25
Machiavelli, Niccolò: 60
Magdelen College: x
Magian culture. SEE culture,
Magian
Mahomet: 64
Mani: 64
Marathon, battle of: 138
Marx, Karl: on materialism, 11, 40,
130
materialism, historical: 11, 40, 130
mathematics, modern: and Greek,
65, 71
"Maud": attitude of, 108
Maximian, Throne of: 79
Melos, massacre of: 84
methods, historical. SEE historiog-
raphy, methods of
Michelangelo: 82
Middle Ages: feudal barbarism in,
65; evidence for, 93; as period of
decline, 112; architecture of,
116; mentioned, 84, 127, 129
Milton, John: 37
Mithras: as Magian, 63
Modern History: 5
Mohammed: 64
Mommsen, Theodor: 11, 14, 139
"Monk's Tale": 17–18
Monumentum Ancryanum: 94
Morris, William: 108
Moses: 76
Muhammad: 64
music: decadence in, 83

Napoleon I: in cyclical theory, 58–
59; mentioned, 115, 148
Neo-Platonists: 64

Neptune: 132
Nero: 100
New Leviathan, The: xi, xxx, xxxi
Newton, Isaac: 81
Nietzsche, Friedrich Wilhelm: 68
nominalists, medieval: 24
Norman Conquest: 38, 43
numismatics: 31, 136

Octavian; 116, 132
Odysseus: 62
Outlines of a Philosophy of Art: xi
Oxford University: Collingwood
at, ix–x, xi; philosophy and
history at, 3, 5; mentioned, 90

paleography: 31, 136
Pantheon: 70, 74, 111
Paradise Lost: 37
Parmenides: 24
Parthenon: 117
particular, the: and history and
science as knowledge, 24–26,
28, 29–30, 113
past, imaginative reconstruction
of: truth of, xvii–xviii; and
authority, xvii, xix; as a priori,
xviii–xix, xxviii; and evidence,
xviii, xix–xx, xxi, xxii; and picture of past, xix–xx, xxi, xxii;
and nature of historical events,
xxvii
Paston Letters: 93, 94
Paton, H. J.: and art in Plato, 23
n. 1
Pembroke College, Oxford: x
perception: history as, 49, 50;
process of, 49–50, 51; interpretation in, 50; past and present experience in, 50–51; and historians' limits, 53–54
Pericles: 114
Peters, R. S.: xxii
Petrie, Sir Flinders: value judg-

Romans: worship of gods by, 62;
progress, 104–105, 107; mentioned, 82
Romantic movement, attitude of:
toward religion, 112; toward history, 133
Rome, ancient: democracy in, 59;
Mithras of, 63; Magian culture
in, 66; overlapping cultures in,
69–70; architecture of, 111, 116,
117; mentioned, 79, 88, 101, 120,
126
Rousseau, Jean Jacques: 107
Rugby School: ix
Ruskin, John: ix, 107–108

St. Andrews University: x, ix
St. Augustine: 125
scepticism, historical: as revisable,
xx–xxi; function of, 43, 91, 99;
validity of, 96–97; effect of, on
historian, 98; relation of, to historical thought, 99–100; in 17th
and 18th century, 127
Schopenhauer, Arthur: progress,
107–108; and history-science distinction, 132–133, 134
science: and study of philosophy,
5; as source of philosophical errors, 12–13; as willing, 18; and
generalizing, 18, 19, 132, 133;
and concern of, with the particular, 19, 27–29, 30, 121–122;
in Aristotle, 23 n. 2; as action,
25; as false knowledge, 25–26;
as utilitarian, 25, 26, 27–28, 28–
29; as activity in mind, 30; and
determination of future, 32, 68;
critical thought and authority in,
32–33; as abstract thought, 45–
46; object of, 45–46, 68; comparison of, with philosophy,
121–122; study of art as, 122;
philosophy of, and Descartes,

127; law-fact relation in, 132;
principles of interpretation as,
136
— and history: comparison of
methods of, xi, xii, xxi–xxii; as
a science, xv, xxxii–xxxiii, 36,
133–134; relationship between,
18–19, 48–49, 131–132, 135–136;
distinction between, 18, 45–46,
132–133; and sciences of history,
25, 31, 52, 136; and universal
histories, 132, 133–134; and science of the individual, 134. SEE
ALSO knowledge, history and science as; scientist
scientist: concern of, with universal, xxxii; generalizations of, 19,
26–29, 132; concern of, with particular, 19, 27–29, 121; and
knowledge of the individual, 30;
"scissors-and-paste" history: process of, xii–xiii, xiv; Collingwood's attitude toward, xii, xiv,
xvii
Scot, John the: 80
sculpture: decadence in, 82, 83;
mentioned, 60
Smollet, Tobias George: on medieval architecture, 78 and n., 79,
87, 88, 89
Social Science: 25
Sociology: 25
Socrates: xxxi, 81
Sol Invictus: 63
sources, historical: as testimony of
authority, xii; criterion for, xiii–
xv; as evidence, xv; nature of,
51, 52; and perception process,
51; criticism of, 51–52; relation
of, to conclusions, 53
— and authority: in "scissors-and-
paste" history, xii–xiv; in Bacon's theory of history, 126; his-

torian's treatment of, 126–127;
and lack of historical method,
129. SEE ALSO evidence
Spain: x
Speculum Mentis: xi
Spencer, Herbert: uniform-to-di-
versified theory of, 130; mentioned, 108, 119
Spengler, Oswald: as historian, 66–
67; on Byzantine art, 80; Goddard and Gibbon's treatment of,
89 n. SEE ALSO *Decline of the
West*
spirit, the, philosophy of. SEE
Croce, Benedetto
Steinthal, Heymann: 134
Stoics: 61
Strauss, Richard: 83
studies, historical. SEE historiography, studies in

Tacitus, Cornelius: 126
Tennyson, Alfred Lord: 108
Teoria e Storia della Storiografia:
Collingwood's review of, xxxii;
theoretical and historical sections of, 5; mentioned, 135. SEE
ALSO Croce, Benedetto
Thierry, Jacques: 11
Thorwaldsen, Bertel: 82
thought: expression of, xxvi–xxviii,
xxix; history as, 6, 7, 9, 10, 18;
and annals, 6, 7; truth of, 6, 12,
14; in "philosophy of the spirit,"
6–7, 8, 9; and error, 10; idealistic
theory of, 9; dualism of, and life,
13–14, 15–16; and history-science distinction, 18; history of,
32, 33; scientific, as abstract, 45–
46; in perception, 50
—, past, re-enactment of: and "inside" of event, xvi, xxiv; and
reason for events, xxii, xxvii–
xxix; conditions for, xxiv–xxvi;

possibility of, xxiv–xxvi; and ex-
pression of thoughts, xxvi–xxviii.
SEE ALSO historiography, and
historical thought
Thucydides: 46, 126
Thutmosis III: as parallel figure,
69
Toynbee, Arnold: xxiii, xxxi
"Truth and Contradiction": xi–xii

universal, the: and history and science as knowledge, 24–26, 28,
29–30, 133
universal history: and self-knowledge of man, xxxi; effect of, on
historical research, 129; refutation of, 130–131; and pattern of
history, 130; and pattern of
logic, 130; merits of, 131; and
history-science relationship, 131;
and law-fact relation, 132; and
concept of genuine knowledge,
133; constructing of, possibility
of, 138
Uranus: 132

Via Appia: 64
Vico, Giambattista: cyclical doctrine of, 57, 60, 72; on barbarism
in cultures, 65; and prophecy,
72; and origin of culture, 72;
and modern philosophy of history, 127; and study of remote
periods, 127; and historical
method, 127–128, 129; on historical error, 128; on Middle
Ages, 130; mentioned, xxxiii, 20,
131
Victoria, Queen: 108
Vikings: 64
Virgil: optimism in, 106, 107
Voltaire: on range of historical
study, 129; philosophy of history
of, 130; mentioned, 131

Printed in the USA
CPSIA information can be obtained
at www.ICGtesting.com
LVHW061359170823
755277LV00008B/816